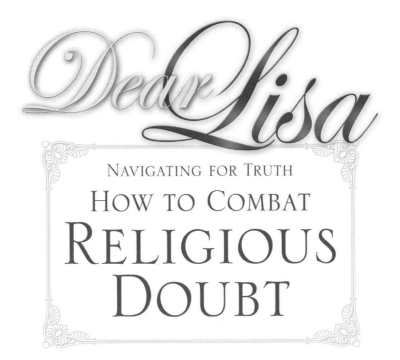

Dear Lisa

Navigating for Truth
How to Combat
Religious Doubt

Gene Burgett

Publishing Designs, Inc.
Huntsville, Alabama

Publishing Designs, Inc.
P.O. Box 3241
Huntsville, Alabama 35810

Printed in the United States

Library of Congress Cataloging-in-Publication Data

Burgett, Gene, 1959-
  Dear Lisa / Gene Burgett.
    p. cm.
  ISBN 0-929540-53-0 (alk. paper)
  1. Apologetics. 2. Imaginary letters. I. Title.
  BT1103.B87 2005
  239—dc22
                          2005024970

DEDICATION

To Cindy,
You're still the one.

CONTENTS

INTRODUCTION

Book titles can be tricky things. Often a title may whet our appetite for one thing while the book may actually be about something entirely different. So let me explain what this book is all about.

I have always been in contact with many people who have not accepted the concept of God as he is set forth in the traditional world religions. These people are not Christians, Hindus, Muslims, or Buddhists, but neither are they atheists. They often describe themselves as spiritual. They have a strong sense of the necessity of good moral conduct and realize the importance of the obligation each of us has to make this world a better place. They believe there is a Higher Power or Presence, but they are dissatisfied with God as they have heard him presented in Christian circles. They may even say, "I believe there is Something out there, but I am not sure how to define that Something." I refer to such people as God-seekers.

The term God-seekers is one I arrived at after much deliberation. In Acts 17:27 Paul said it was God's desire that all people should seek him, but he described some as seeking him like a blind man feels or gropes his way around. Now the term *gropers* or *feelers* sounded decidedly unflattering. *God-seekers* won by default.

This book is a series of letters between me and a God-seeker named Lisa. Lisa is actually a composite of the many God-seekers I have met, not a personal acquaintance.

Who might benefit from this work? One obvious group is seekers. The forces rallied against Christianity are running a rather successful disinformation campaign. Many who fancy they are rejecting Christianity aren't actually rebelling against what Jesus taught. Instead they are opposed to what someone has wrongly told them Jesus taught. The discrediting example of some Christians often contributes to the problem. I desire to at least set the record straight, allowing the seeker to accept or reject an accurate portrayal of Christianity.

But more than any other, Christians will derive the greatest benefit from this work. Christians are charged always to be "ready to make a defense to everyone who asks you to give an account for the hope that is in you, yet with gentleness and reverence" (1 Peter 3:15 NASB). This book is to help equip Christians to meet that obligation.

This work sets forth many of the questions seekers are asking, for they aren't always the questions Christians are accustomed to answering. Our usual concept of a religious discussion involves someone that already has a fairly accurate view of the Bible as being the word of God and Jesus as being the divine Son of God. Our usual exchange begins with topics like how to be saved, the identity of the church, or whether or not one can fall from grace. But the world we live in is a bit more skeptical than it once was. Now we must often prove that the biblical concept of God is the correct concept.

It is also my desire to address with *brevity* the questions seekers are asking. In addressing the concerns of seekers, Christians may feel as if they are expected to be experts in the minute details of religion, science, ancient languages, and archaeology. This is, in part, because much of the discussion that takes place about issues important to seekers is really about peripheral matters. I have refrained from getting lost in the peripheral details, confining my responses to the nucleus of the question that is being addressed. This makes for brief but convincing answers.

Finally, I have chosen this correspondence format for the book so that I might write in the second person. My desire is to create an atmosphere that sounds more like two people chatting about the weather or the condition of the wallpaper, rather than saying things like, "Now *they* believe this or that." None of us likes to be referred to in the third person. It is a bit like being a party to a conversation that is wholly about you, but the speakers act as if you weren't in the room. My hope is that the responses in the dialogue of the book have the gentle tone Peter called for when Christians "give an answer."

HOW TO USE THIS BOOK

This book is written to be used in two ways. One may simply read it from beginning to end as a series of letters. Reading the book in this fashion allows one to become acquainted with the relationship of the two main characters as the correspondence develops and as their lives unfold in the letters.

On the other hand, the busy Bible class teacher may not be interested in the entertainment value associated with the development of the characters. For this reason the contents reveals the 13-part division of the material covered as well as the specific topics addressed, making it possible to use the book in a Bible class without the story line, or even as a reference work.

To any seekers who read this work: This book is a presentation of Christianity. It is an attempt to answer questions and address issues that the many God-seekers I have met in life have raised. If I fail to be convincing, then my hope is that you will keep seeking him.

1

What Is Truth?

THE SEARCH BEGINS

Chartings

- Intellectual Laziness
- False Information
- Flawed Christianity
- Nagging Doubts
- Hypocrisy vs. Mistakes

October 2

Dear Lisa,

During the past year we have had quite a few conversations about religion and life philosophy in general. I have really enjoyed and benefited from our conversations. But I am always left with the feeling we didn't really finish what we started, and there is always uncertainty as to when we will be able to talk again. Besides, it is almost impossible to really pick up where you left off. For those reasons I have taken the liberty of beginning this written correspondence with you. I hope I am not being too forward about this, but our conversations have convinced me that you really are interested in spiritual matters, so we might as well dig in and see if together we can solve some of these dilemmas.

As you know, I am a Christian and I believe Christianity is the answer for people seeking God. But you have mentioned several times you are reluctant to accept Christianity as a means of finding

God. What is it specifically about the Movement that makes you so hesitant to accept its teachings?

There are several possible answers to this question. Maybe some of the presentations you have seen of Christianity have been flawed. The flaw may be, to put it simply, that someone got it wrong. Unfortunately, many "Christians" really don't understand what Christianity teaches. Some of our more zealous advocates are not among our best informed. Some people refuse to allow their own ignorance to keep them down, even when it really should.

Another possibility is that some of the Christian conduct you have witnessed has been defective. When a person professes to be of a certain conviction, it is only natural that people should begin to look at him to see what kind of people are of the conviction he professes. When the one making a certain profession behaves badly, the profession is tainted. This is especially true when a person says he acted with the approval, or even at the instigation of God. This inevitably seems to lead to the charge of hypocrisy. For this reason the Bible itself often urges Christians to behave themselves properly so as not to bring shame on the name of Jesus Christ (1 Peter 4:12–19; 1 Timothy 6:1).

I offer no defense for poor behavior on the part of any of my fellow Christians. My own behavior is sometimes all too short of what I proclaim. But I hope as you consider these examples of poor conduct, you are willing to differentiate between sincere people making mistakes (sometimes even bad mistakes), and insincere people who are pretending to be something they are not.

Here is another word of caution. To invalidate an entire religious system based on your knowledge of the conduct of some of its followers may be a sign of intellectual laziness. To say you saw several Christians misbehave is not the same as actually studying what Jesus taught about Christian behavior.

I wish everything you find objectionable about Christianity is simply representations that do not accurately portray what Jesus taught; however, I realize that is too much to hope for. I am certain some of the things you find objectionable reflect true Christian teaching. The best I can hope for is to offer some thoughts from a different perspective—the kind of thing where you say, "I never thought of it quite that way before."

Be assured, I have no intention of changing the teachings of Christianity to make it more acceptable. I believe I have an obligation to both you and God. I must present Christianity as I have come to believe it—the only way we can honestly present anything—because I believe God would have it no other way. Jesus himself had no desire to gain followers under false pretenses. That is why some of his speeches left him with fewer rather than more followers (John 6:60–71).

My obligation to you, Lisa, rises from my conviction that no decision should ever be based on false information. Your quest for God is the most important thing you have to do in your life. You should not be lied to.

One final word: In matters as important as these, few people become convinced in one great cataclysmic moment. I hear a lot about that great moment when the whole thing suddenly made sense—when one previously skeptical of Christianity came to accept the entire teachings of Jesus in the twinkling of an eye. But for most of us (certainly for me) accepting is a process. It takes a while because some things are more readily received than others. Many become Christians though nagging doubts may remain about some aspects of Jesus' teachings. Some may even accept a little begrudgingly. That is only natural. Some of what Jesus taught runs contrary to personal desires. But most mature people realize that what we want (desire) is not always what's best for us. Being a Christian is a continual process of growing and not an action one completes in a moment (2 Peter 3:18).

The biggest mistake seekers can make is to end their examination prematurely. The nagging little doubts often go away as one's understanding grows more complete. Truth comes in small bits like pieces of a jigsaw puzzle that, by themselves, don't look like much, but together make perfect sense. The problem is, many people don't stick around long enough to see the whole picture.

I hope to hear from you soon.

Your friend,
Gene

SOUNDINGS

1. Is one a hypocrite just because he does or teaches something that is wrong? Defend your answer.

2. When someone questions Christianity, why should we consider his circumstance before responding? Contrast the way Paul answered the people of Athens (Acts 17:16–34) with the way he answered those in Acts 13:42–47.

3. An example of intellectual laziness is (a) examining a religious movement (b) examining the conduct of a person from a religious movement.

HOW PREJUDICE HIDES GOD

Chartings

Truth, Not Feeling

A God Like Me

Preconceived Ideas

Judging God

October 7

Dear Lisa,

Thanks for replying to my letter.

I did not realize you had been thinking seriously about spiritual matters for such a long time. I understand why, in view of your long search, you feel there really isn't any one true way to find God.

Sometimes the secret to finding something is not in how hard we look, but in how we look. This is especially true when we are looking for something and we are only vaguely aware of what it looks like. We get a picture in our mind of what the thing looks like, but if our picture is wrong, then it really messes everything up. We could be staring at the real thing without recognizing it.

Most of us—especially men—have had the rather embarrassing experience of claiming a certain item was not in a kitchen cabinet, only to have it later produced from that same cabinet, usually by our wives. Often the problem was we were looking for a red label when the label was actually blue. Our own expectation of what the item should look like actually prevented our finding it.

One reason Jesus was rejected was because he did not fit the preconceived idea as to how the Messiah should look and act. Those who crucified him had expected the Messiah to establish a physical kingdom and rule over it as an earthly monarch. On one occasion they even tried to "take him by force and make him a king," but he refused (John 6:15). God doesn't always act the way we think he should, which is a good thing. Unfortunately, determining in our minds how God ought to act increases the difficulty of our finding him.

I admire you because you are a caring and loving person. Injustices really get you worked up because you have a well-defined sense of justice. Though you claim to have a rather vague concept of God, you may have a more definite idea of God than you realize. God, by definition, is a loving and caring Being who champions the cause of the weak when they are trampled by the strong. Like you, he loves justice and hates injustice.

Since you already have very strong ideas about important matters such as love, justice, and the importance of looking to the needs of others, I suspect you are looking for a God who shares your ideas on these matters. In other words, you have an idea of the color of the label. You have certain expectations of how God ought to believe and behave, and any view of God that does not meet your expectations is likely going to be rejected. There is a biblical story that illustrates that very concept. (Read 2 Kings 5.)

Lisa, please don't be insulted, but what if at least some of your ideas about love, justice, and morality are wrong? What if something you consider to be an injustice is really not unjust at all? What if a certain behavior that, in your mind, is the loving thing to do really isn't loving at all? I know that is hard to imagine. Because of your passions about such things, it is difficult to believe you could be that far off. But if you are wrong about at least some of these matters, it would mean God might look considerably different from what you imagined. This much I know: if the movie depictions reveal the concept people have of the Almighty, the true God is very differ-ent from what they seek. He is not anything like Bruce Almighty or George Burns.

There is a temptation to say, "I just can't believe I could be that far off about these things." That is a stronger statement than you may realize. It really amounts to a claim of omniscience. It is set-ting oneself up as being capable of judging God, and that is a pretty lofty position. The biblical teaching is that God is high above man, so God's ways and thoughts are not always in agreement with ours (Isaiah 55:8–9; Jeremiah 10:23). We simply cannot assume that the correct concept of God is the one we have created independently in our mind.

The search for God is a search for truth, not for a Supreme Being who believes like me. You and I have discussed the concept of truth on a number of occasions. There is a lot of disagreement about what truth is, and whether or not it can really be known. Some believe it is possible for something to be both true and not true at the same time and in the same way. That makes for nice philosophical discussion, but creates havoc when applied to real life situations. That's why many people who espouse certain ideas about truth do not actually live by those ideas. People often speak of "the truth as you see it" when referring to religious matters. However, when it comes to the day-to-day decisions of life, such a concept isn't very practical.

Are you ready for a really profound idea? Here it is: if something is true, then it is true. Now I am sure that is a rather disappointing statement considering the build-up it received. But that idea is im-portant because it takes truth out of the realm of how I feel about something and makes it objective, rather than subjective. And here is something else that is great about that idea concerning truth: deep down we all really believe it because we live by it in the normal af-fairs of life.

A few months ago you got a new car. Your car is white, as I recall. Now why is your car white? Is it white because I believe it is white? No, it is white because it is white. White is its color. Now when you went to pick your car up from the dealer, if they had brought out a red one you would have said something like, "Hey, that's not the car I ordered. I ordered a white car and that one is red." And if the salesman had said to you, "Well, to me that car is white," you would not have thought for a moment he might be right. It wouldn't have mattered how the salesman felt about the color of the car, because if it is red then it is red. And if it is red then it can't be white. It can't be both (assuming we aren't talking about a two-tone paint job).

That is how we deal with truth in the normal affairs of life, and things could get pretty hectic if people acted differently. Since we hold to this rather practical view of truth daily, I see no reason we should suddenly get impractical about religious truth. If something is true, then it is true.

Isn't simplicity wonderful!

Your friend,
Gene

SOUNDINGS

1. Discuss the effect of Naaman's preconceived expectations on his responses to the prophet's command (2 Kings 5:9–14).

2. What, if anything, is wrong with that statement "truth as you see it"?

3. What factor or factors make learning the truth difficult?

EXAMINING CHRISTIANITY
MEANS EXAMINING JESUS

Chartings

Wrong Places

Behavior

Claims

Issues

October 12

Dear Lisa,

In your last letter you mentioned your mother has been sick. Is she better? If there is something I can do to help, please let me know.

I was intrigued by your comment that it seems strange to you God should be so difficult to find. You wonder why he doesn't make himself more obvious.

Let me make an alternate suggestion to your hypothesis that God is hard to find. No search can be successful if the searcher is looking in the wrong place. If you want to find fish you must look in the water. If you are looking in the desert for fish, you are not more likely to find them just by looking harder. The diligence of the search is not the problem. It goes without saying that we cannot blame the fish, because we are looking in the wrong place. Neither should we blame God when we cannot find him if we are looking in the wrong place.

Many God-seekers are looking in the wrong places for him. Some who have rejected Christianity—often called "organized religion"—aren't necessarily rejecting the teachings of Jesus. They may not know the teachings of Jesus. They are irked at some who claim to be his followers. They are rejecting the guy who bombs abortion clinics, the preacher caught in a money scandal, or the Sunday school teacher accused of molesting children. Many do horrible things in the name of Jesus, but that doesn't mean Jesus approves of their actions. The point is, you won't find Jesus by looking at the conduct of a few nuts who claim to be his followers.

Many of your objections to Christianity have to do with issues. That is not unusual. Many people say they could never accept the Christian faith because of its views on abortion, capital punishment, gender roles, sexual conduct, or even the environment.

Perhaps you have received misinformation about Christianity, but there is a more fundamental matter: this is really just another example of looking for God in the wrong place. You really can't begin searching for God by looking at issues. It is like saying, "I'll know when someone is teaching the truth about God because it will look just like my concept of God." Should we make ourselves the standard by which God is judged?

The truthfulness of Christianity is based on whether or not the claims Jesus made about himself are true. The Bible teaches that in Jesus, God "became flesh and dwelt among us" (John 1:1–3, 14). One of the men who wrote about the life of Jesus specifically said it was his aim to prove "Jesus is the Christ" (John 20:30–31). If Jesus was God, then any disagreements we have with him are settled. What could you possibly say to him? "Sir, I know you are divine but there are a couple of things you taught with which I must take issue." That is not very likely.

If Jesus is not who he claimed to be, then why consider Christianity at all? If he wasn't who he said he was, then the entire Christian movement is built on a guy who was either a lunatic who thought he was God or a liar who wanted people to believe he was God. Neither option inspires great confidence.

Look at it this way. If you are looking for a bottle of medicine the logical place to first look is the medicine cabinet. If it isn't there, then look somewhere else. The logical place to begin examining Christianity is Jesus, and the only detailed information we have about Jesus is in the Gospels—Matthew, Mark, Luke, and John. If you are really interested in determining whether or not Christianity is the correct concept of God, then read what those who knew him best wrote about him. If after looking at the person of Jesus you still aren't satisfied, then look somewhere else.

Your friend,
Gene

SOUNDINGS

1. Among the people who reject Christianity, what percentage has actually read the Bible?

2. If people reject Christianity without having read the Bible, what might be the basis for their rejection?

3. In Romans 1:18–25 Paul condemns people who rejected knowledge of God as he is revealed in nature. How does nature point to the existence of God? What can we know about God from nature?

2

Things That Hinder a Search for Truth

OVERCOMING THE BAD EXAMPLE OF SOME BELIEVERS

Chartings

• **Offenses**

• **Encounters**

• **Churches**

• **Focus**

October 19

Dear Lisa,

I am very sorry to hear of your recent experience with a church-going person. I wish I could say yours is the first case where a professing Christian did someone a nasty turn, but it's not. I do hope you can get your money back. I also hope that individual turns away from that kind of behavior. Eventually they will encounter the One who said, "Woe to the world because of offenses! For offenses must come, but woe to that man by whom the offense comes!" (Matthew 18:7). A Christian should conduct himself in such a way as to cause others to glorify God (Matthew 5:13–16).

At the risk of sounding unsympathetic, I have a question for you: Do you think it is wise to dismiss organized religion because of your bad experience? I am aware that many people offer this reason for rejecting churches; I simply question the prudence of such a line of thought.

Many people have had an unpleasant encounter with a doctor, but when they get sick they still seek a physician. Why would a person continue to trust the medical profession after a bad experience? First, because we all know that one bad doctor is not representative of all doctors. Most of them are really quite nice and want to see their patients in good health. And second, because they continue to have confidence in the factual basis of medicine. If the behavior of the naughty doctor somehow proved the whole body of medical knowledge is hocus-pocus, then all would do well to avoid the medical profession. But the fact that certain medical practices, procedures, and therapies are beneficial to our health is not invalidated by a doctor's bad behavior. Quite simply, even if a doctor did you wrong, it is still a good idea to have an inflamed appendix removed.

I hope you will keep your focus on whether or not Christianity is true, rather than on the behavior of a few people who claim to be followers. If Jesus was who he said he was, the bad behavior of some who say they follow him doesn't change that truth. If the Bible is a revelation of the mind of God, bad behavior on the part of believers doesn't invalidate it. These are the two areas upon which the validity of Christianity rests. It is also one's conclusion about these two matters that ought to determine whether or not one becomes a Christian.

I regret your bad experience, but let me assure you this individual behaved as he did despite going to church, not because he goes to church. To reject Christianity because some who profess it misbehave seems to assume it was in a church they learned the behavior. One almost gets the impression that churches are like Fagin in Charles Dickens' *Oliver*. Fagin collected abandoned street kids and turned them into an army of thieves and pick-pockets. That is not what churches are all about. One of the things churches are supposed to do is encourage honest and upright conduct among their people, even to the point of withdrawing from those that behave badly (1 Corinthians 5).

In a weird way you have actually made an argument for church attendance. You seem to be saying you don't want to go to church because some of the people who attend are of poor character. If it is association with bad people you seek to avoid, then you really ought to go to church. I think I can safely say there are more evil people outside churches than in them.

Your friend,
Gene

SOUNDINGS

1. What would be the result if everyone in your town rejected the police department because some on the force abuse their positions?

2. How does our focus on finding truth keep us from being fooled by others' behavior?

3. How can you encourage truth seekers in spite of misbehaving church members?

WILL BECOMING A CHRISTIAN MAKE ONE HAPPIER?

Chartings

- Why Believe?
- Fantasy vs. Reality
- Myth of Easy Life
- Knowing Truth

October 26

Dear Lisa,

If my reply seems to lack continuity, please attribute it to sleep depravation. Our son had a birthday sleep-over that ended yesterday, and seven rousing ten-year-old boys in a house don't leave much room for sleep.

Do I think you would be happier by believing in Christianity? I am not sure why you are asking. Will my answer be the deciding factor in whether or not you believe? I hope not. The only reason one ought to believe anything is because it is true.

Neither am I sure what you mean by happier. Many believe that being happier means having an easier life—a life without problems. Happiness means good health. Happiness means having an enjoyable job that pays a lot. Happiness means financial plenty. If these are the kinds of things you mean when you ask if you will be happier for believing in Christianity, then I am unable to answer your question. Honestly, you and Blaine appear pretty happy already by these measures. Let me be clear: Jesus never promised his followers they would have an easy life. He often taught them to expect treatment similar to the treatment he received (Matthew 10:21–25; John 15:18–21).

I have never recommended that anyone become a Christian in order to maximize happiness. That which most call happiness is better found in a religion that encourages one to fulfill personal desires. In the short term, which is really what happiness is all about, no religion at all may be preferred. That also seemed to be the understanding of the apostle Paul, who wrote the majority of the New Testament and may have been Christianity's greatest defender. He once stated that if the basis for believing in Christianity is not true, then "let us eat and drink, for tomorrow we die" (1 Corinthians 15:32).

I believe you would be happier as a Christian because the teachings of Christianity are true. Jesus really is the Son of God, and in becoming a Christian you are recognizing that truth. Jesus truly said it is truth that sets us free (John 8:32).

The kind of happiness that results from knowing the truth is often quite different from the feel-good kind we usually have in mind. In fact, truth may make us feel a bit worse at the outset. And, whether or not truth ever produces any beneficial results depends on what one does with it.

A person with a drinking problem usually feels better after having a drink. But any time you mistake the problem for the solution, you are going to end up with disaster. On the other hand, what happens when those who drink learn that drinking is their problem and ceasing to drink is the solution? They have opened themselves up to some very difficult days in the near future should they decide to act on that truth. But that same truth is the only hope they have to a greater happiness.

Accepting Christianity may initially result in difficult days of adjusting to life as a believer. One must face the *thou shalts* and the *thou shalt nots*. It may even result in family pressures (Matthew 10:34–39). But dark days surely lie ahead for those who never adjust their lives to reality. Fantasies are nice while one is asleep, but it would never do to walk around living that way in the real world.

The happiness of Christianity is the kind that comes from knowing the truth.

Your friend,
Gene

SOUNDINGS

1. Has the truth ever brought you misery? Were you better for knowing the truth despite the pain?

2. Relate the importance of truth to decision making. Can it be harmful for us to make a decision based on a lie? (cf. Romans 1:24–32).

3. Some believe that what we don't know can't hurt us. Discuss in view of 1 Kings 13.

IS JESUS THE ONLY WAY TO THE FATHER?

Chartings

Exclusive Way

Forgiveness

Divine Leader

Many Religions

Hurt Feelings

November 1

Dear Lisa,

Yes, it is true. Jesus did say he is the exclusive way to salvation and eternity with God. The exact statement you are looking for is found in John 14:6: "I am the way, the truth, and the life. No one comes to the Father except through me."

I understand the tendency to react negatively to this statement. It certainly is saying that God does not approve of religions other than the one founded by Jesus. I know that idea is offensive to many people, since they believe it paints an unloving picture of an intolerant God who will not accept the religion of the many Muslims, Buddhists, and Hindus.

It will be difficult to get away from the emotional aspects of this subject, but let's try for just a moment. Rather than asking whether Jesus' claim is unloving or harsh, a better question would be, is it true? Furthermore, it would be unloving for Jesus to remain silent if one could be pleasing to God only by being one of his followers.

Part of the problem with Jesus' statement is the idea that the sincerity of people following other religious leaders is being questioned. But Jesus is not doubting anyone's sincerity. He speaks a simple truth: "No one comes to the Father except through me."

Lisa, if this statement is true, then the loving thing to do is to make the truth known, even if it hurts someone's feelings. Look at it this way. Suppose a boy in your seventh grade science class has been working really hard on a project. He has really thrown himself into it. But when you examine his project you realize that despite his diligence, he is doing it all wrong. What should you do? Keep silent in order not to hurt his feelings, knowing that the project will later receive a poor grade, or warn him about his mistake so he may correct it? We both know the loving thing for you to do.

It is important to understand this situation in the larger context of who Jesus was and what he did. The biblical teaching is that God wanted to offer forgiveness to the human race. But the only way to accomplish forgiveness was for God to let another stand in the place of all human beings and accept the punishment for their crimes. This meant finding someone who was guilt-free, and the only person who fit that description was Jesus (Hebrews 4:15). So John tells us: "For God so loved the world that He gave His only begotten Son" (John 3:16).

If salvation can be found by means of following the teachings of other religious leaders, then it must also follow that Jesus did not have to die, as there were other options that would produce salvation for humanity. If this were true, the sacrifice of Jesus would stand as one of the most unloving actions of all time. The Father had allowed his only Son to be tortured unnecessarily. If you had a child, would you be willing to sacrifice it unnecessarily?

Why can the Father be found only by accepting Jesus? Because Jesus is the Son of God. The founders of other religious movements may have had many wonderful qualities, but none of them claimed such a lofty position. If it is true that Jesus is divine, wouldn't you

find it odd that one could obtain the same promises he offered through the teachings of someone else?

Believe me, I understand the difficulty involved here. But our quest for God places a premium on recognizing what is true. If it is true that Jesus was God in the flesh, then how can we imagine following anyone else could be just as good?

Your friend,
Gene

SOUNDINGS

1. Which had you rather receive: (a) necessary correction or (b) false flattery? Why?

2. How can obeying the teachings of a mere man obtain the same result as obeying the Son of God, who claims to be divine?

3. How should you respond to the following: "I think there are many ways to the Father. After all, some unbelievers uphold a higher moral standard than some believers"?

WHAT IS FAITH?

Chartings

Definition

Testimonial

Cause-Effect

November 5

Evidence

Dear Lisa,

I'll bet if we were to do a word association study, we would find that when most people hear the word *faith*, they immediately associate it with religion. However, connecting faith with religion and connecting it correctly with religion are not at all the same. Many religious people have accepted an unbiblical definition of faith. I think this may be one of those situations where you have received misinformation about biblical teachings.

What does it mean to accept something by faith? The common idea is that faith is belief without knowledge, an emotional leap in the dark that goes against all reason and sound judgment.

Many religious people seem to substantiate this mistaken concept of faith when they respond to challenges to their beliefs with statements such as, "You just have to believe." If that is the extent of the evidence they can muster, then it is no wonder Christianity looks rather silly to many people.

Biblically speaking, faith is not belief without knowledge. It is belief without sight. The Bible says, "For we walk by faith, not by sight" (2 Corinthians 5:7). Faith is not belief in the unbelievable; it is belief in something that cannot be seen. It is not knowledge faith is missing; it is sight. Since many of the concepts central to Christianity cannot be seen with the physical eye, it is faith that gives them substance. "Now faith is the substance of things hoped for, the evidence of things not seen" (Hebrews 11:1). The Bible does not encourage people to be irrational or to accept things without adequate evidence. On the contrary, the Bible teaches Christians to "test all things; hold fast what is good" (1 Thessalonians 5:21).

We believe in many things we have never personally seen. The evidence for such belief is testimonial and cause-effect.

Testimonial evidence is the basis for much of our belief in historical events. Testimonial evidence is based on someone's account of an event. The testimony usually originates as an oral statement that is later committed to writing. Historical documents are a form of testimonial evidence.

The second form of evidence that leads us to believe in things we can't see is cause and effect. We believe in gravity because we see its effect, but we can't actually see gravity. None of us has seen a dinosaur, but their fossils are evidence that they once existed. We believe in the cause (dinosaurs) because of their effect (fossil remains).

Our belief in the existence of God is based on cause-effect evidence. We can't see God, but we can see a creation that demands a Creator.

Our belief in Jesus is based on testimonial evidence, especially the testimonies of Matthew, Mark, Luke, and John, the writers of the first four books of the New Testament.

Christians are not expected to believe in the unbelievable. By faith Christians do believe in things they can't see. But then, don't we all believe in things we've never seen?

Your friend,
Gene

SOUNDINGS

1. Name some commonly accepted concepts of which most have no tangible experience or evidence?

2. The Bible teaches "no one has seen God at any time" (John 1:18). Since we have not seen God, what evidence leads us to believe there is a God? (cf. Romans 1:18–20).

3. Can we trust the things we accept by faith with a hundred percent certainty? If not, to what degree can we trust matters of faith?

3

Deity of Jesus
CAN WE KNOW GOD?

Chartings

- Private Thoughts
- Higher Ways
- Learn God's Character
- Silent God?

November 10

Dear Lisa,

I am glad you believe in God but don't you find it alarming that you have serious doubts as to whether or not it is possible to know anything about him? I would find it quite distressing if I thought there was a God, but I had no way of knowing anything about the ways, plans, and thoughts of that Being. It would be like finding out I had a sister I didn't know existed. I would not be content with merely knowing she existed; I would want to know something about her. I would be full of questions. What is her name? Where does she live? Is she married? Does she have any children? Does she know I exist? Of course, more than anything else, I would want to meet her. I would want to get to know her. I would want to learn of her character.

Several of the authors of the Bible raised the very question you recently mentioned: Is it possible to know God? The prophet Isaiah paints a rather discouraging picture of our ability to know God simply through our own mental efforts. Isaiah said of God: 'For my thoughts are not your thoughts, nor are your ways my ways,' says the Lord. 'For as the heavens are higher than the earth, so are my ways higher than your ways, and my thoughts than your thoughts'" (Isaiah 55:8–9).

In the New Testament the apostle Paul noted that this problem is not exclusively a problem with knowing God. It is even difficult to know the thoughts of our fellow human beings. First Corinthians 2:11 says, "For who among men know the thoughts of a man except the spirit of the man, which is in him?" (NASB). Every time we hear someone express surprise that "George would do that," we have just received confirmation that the private thoughts of another are a mystery. If we cannot know the private thoughts of a close friend, it is no wonder that we question the possibility of knowing the mind of God.

We can get some idea of what others believe by observing their behavior, but even then things get a bit tricky. Behavior is subject to various motivations; it is often a slave of the moment. A few years ago I had an acquaintance whom I saw only a couple of times a year when we both visited his parents. It seemed that every time I saw him he was wearing the same shirt. I naturally assumed it was among his favorites. Later he told me he disliked the shirt very much, but it was a gift from his parents. He wore it only when he visited them. That man's behavior didn't reveal his true feelings, not about the shirt, anyway, though he must have loved his parents very much.

I learned my friend's true opinion of the shirt because he chose to reveal it to me. That is exactly where Paul was going when he asked if anyone could know a person's thoughts other than the person himself. Paul claimed that God was revealing his thoughts to the apostles. "Even so the thoughts of God no one knows except the Spirit of God." Paul then says that he and the other apostles had been given the Spirit of God so they might know the will of God and tell it to others (1 Corinthians 2:11–13 NASB).

Anyone can claim to be revealing the will of God, so what made the apostle's assertion credible? The answer is miracles. Miracles were God's way of "bearing witness" to the veracity of the speaker (Hebrews 2:3–4).

The Bible claims to be the thoughts of God, and that is what Christians mean when they refer to it as the word of God. We believe that through the Bible God is telling us what's on his mind. So to answer your question, "Can we know God?" the answer is yes. The Bible is a revelation of the mind of God. Bible writers claimed to be speaking and writing the very words of God (2 Timothy 3:16–17). Paul once commended a group of people because when they heard his teaching they "welcomed it not as the word of men, but as it is in truth, the word of God" (1 Thessalonians 2:13).

The idea of a Supreme Being that chooses not to communicate with his creation is one that strikes me as very odd. It would be something like a parent refusing to speak to his child. When you consider that we humans, made in the image of God, will talk to fellow human beings and everything else from the family pet to a car—especially when it won't start—a silent God seems incredible.

Your friend,
Gene

SOUNDINGS

1. What do most people mean when they talk about knowing God?

2. Have you ever been surprised by the behavior or beliefs of a person you thought you knew very well? If yes, what did you learn from that experience?

3. Read the following passages: John 17:3; Titus. 1:16; Galatians 4:8–9. What do they teach pertaining to knowledge of God?

4. Can we come to know God by means of our own intellect or do we need a revelation from God? (cf. 1 Corinthians. 1:21). Explain your answer.

DID JESUS REALLY EXIST?

Chartings

• **Make Believe?**

• **Limited View**

• **Historians**

• **Evidence**

November 14

Dear Lisa,

I enjoyed reading your letter very much. Thank you for the picture of your cat and her new kittens. I am afraid I must decline your gracious offer to give me one of the kittens. I am allergic to the little beasts.

Regarding your question, is it possible to know if a man named Jesus really existed, let me assure you we can. There is plenty of evidence that Jesus was a real person who lived in the first-century Roman Empire. There really is very little debate on this matter. If nothing else, the New Testament is a valuable historical reference to that fact.

In your letter you wonder if the New Testament should be regarded as a legitimate source about the life of Jesus, since its authors were part of the early Christian movement. If you are saying that the New Testament writers made up the story of Jesus, then you are making a very serious accusation. What about them causes you to think they would do such a thing?

Even if we did not have the New Testament, there would be no doubt that a Jewish religious leader named Jesus was crucified outside Jerusalem in the first century. Several first- and second-century writers made references to Jesus and the Christian movement. Some of the writers were historians and some were politicians. Some were bitter enemies of the Christian movement.

A first-century Jewish historian named Flavius Josephus (A.D. 37–100) wrote about many famous events and people of his day. In one of his works he wrote of "the brother of Jesus, the so-called Christ, whose name was James" (Antiquities XX 9:1).

Another first-century Roman historian, Cornelius Tacitus, mentioned Jesus. Tacitus explains that when the city of Rome burned, Nero "falsely charged with the guilt, and punished with the most exquisite tortures, the persons commonly called Christians, who were hated for their enormities. Christus, the founder of the name, was put to death by Pontius Pilate, procurator of Judea in the reign of Tiberius" (Annals XV. 44).

An early second-century governor, Pliny the Younger (circa. A.D. 112), described Christians as people who "were in the habit of meeting on a certain fixed day before it was light, when they sang in alternate verse a hymn to Christ as to a god, and bound themselves to a solemn oath, not to do any wicked deeds, and never to deny a truth when they should be called upon to deliver it up" (Epistles X. 96). Pliny wrote a letter to the emperor asking what he should do with the Christians. (He had already killed many of them.)

A Samaritan-born historian named Thallus (A.D. 52) even tried to explain the darkness that occurred during the crucifixion of Jesus "as an eclipse of the sun."

Lisa, I can give you other historical references to Jesus should you desire further research. However, I consider the above evidence sufficient to confidently state: Jesus did live. The more important question is, was Jesus who he said he was? Was he God in the flesh? If so, accepting Jesus' will is the natural thing to do.

Many people are put off in their search for God because they see him as a bit incomprehensible. Part of our problem in trying to understand God is our limited view of the universe. Our view of understanding God is kind of like an ant's view of his domain. To us a blade of grass is something to be stepped on. To an ant that same blade of grass must be climbed. To us trees are for climbing, but I can't even imagine what a tree must look like to an ant. Though ants do climb trees, do you think they have any concept of what the whole thing looks like? I doubt it. Their view of the whole is too limited. It is like the difference in our seeing a forest while walking through it and while flying over it. A house in the middle of the forest may be easily seen from above, but locating it on foot is a different thing.

We are part of God's creation trying to understand the Creator. Trying to understand things you are a part of is bound to be difficult. I suspect if we could view the universe from outside it—seeing all of the present, past, and future—things might look much different from how we ever imagined. My point is, don't let your questions about the nature of God keep you from him. If you had no unanswered questions, that would really be odd! An all-knowing, all-powerful, omnipresent Being is rather unique. Does it really seem so strange that we might not understand everything about him?

Your friend,
Gene

SOUNDINGS

1. What proof can you give of the existence of Jesus?

2. How would your beliefs change if you learned that a man named Jesus never existed?

3. Is it reasonable to disbelieve a religion because it doesn't explain all the questions about the universe? Are some questions too big for us to understand? Explain your answers.

WAS JESUS MERELY A HOLY MAN?

Chartings

- Moral Leader
- Character Counts
- No Middle Ground
- Messiah
- Blasphemy

November 19

Dear Lisa,

I find it interesting that most people who take the time to read what Jesus taught are favorably impressed. So I was not surprised to learn of your favorable view of Jesus as a moral leader and teacher. Many people who do not accept the divinity of Jesus refer to him as a holy man, a great religious leader, or the founder of an exceptional code of morality. Many of Jesus' contemporaries felt the same way. While there were a few in the rival religious parties that claimed he had a demon, most who heard him had a favorable opinion. On one occasion Jesus asked his disciples what the people were saying about him. The general consensus was that he was a prophet (Matthew 16:13–20).

Now all of that is very nice, but Jesus' teachings encompassed more than a code of moral conduct. Jesus also made the personal claim that he was the long awaited Messiah predicted by the Hebrew prophets. To claim to be the Messiah was to assert one's deity, for the prophets said the Messiah would be divine. The Messiah would be called "Mighty God" and "Everlasting Father" (Isaiah 9:6). So Jesus claimed to be more than a great moral teacher or a holy man; he said he was God.

When Jesus said he was God, it wasn't merely a slip of the tongue during an unguarded moment. He made or accepted this claim repeatedly before both friendly and hostile gatherings. He said Peter was blessed for recognizing that he was the Christ (the Greek word for Messiah), and he didn't back away from the idea while he was among those who considered such a claim a blasphemy worthy of death if made falsely (Matthew 16:16–17; John 5:17–18).

In making this claim Jesus has placed us in a rather awkward position. Most unbelievers consider it a great compliment when they grant that Jesus was a great moral teacher and a holy man, but those titles are insults in the face of his claim to be God. When you say of God that he was a good moral teacher, it is a bit like saying Einstein was a scientist who knew a little about physics, or Michael Jordan is a guy who played a little basketball. It is a huge understatement. Lisa, any opinion you form about Jesus' character must consider not only his code of human conduct but also his personal claims of deity.

Suppose you knew a man, widely proclaimed to be *the* expert on what it means to be a good husband, who busied himself lecturing on the subject. His presence packed lecture halls across the country. Then the truth comes out: this man has been beating his wife regularly for years. Would you honor him as a great man and teacher on how to treat one's wife? Of course not! Character does count.

Jesus said he was God, and that claim has to be a part of one's opinion about him. If you accept his claim, then becoming one of his followers is the natural result.

You may reject Jesus' claim to be God, but the claim must still be included in your view of him. One explanation may be that he lied when he said he was God. If this is your conclusion, then you must keep in mind that he was not your ordinary run-of-the-mill liar. He told a whopper and he told it repeatedly. He also managed to convince a lot of people that he was God, and many of these people suffered greatly for it. Jesus becomes positively monstrous in this case, and it is hardly possible to say he was a holy man and a great moral teacher if in fact he were a liar.

Another option is that one could conclude he was a nut. And not just a little nutty, mind you. He was stark raving mad because he believed he was God. I would find it quite unsettling to believe a huge portion of the world population is recommending we live by a moral code generated by a lunatic. When one reads what Jesus taught, the idea that he was maniacal is pretty difficult to accept.

So Lisa, Jesus has placed us in a position where we cannot dismiss him lightly as one of a great succession of religious/moral leaders. He seems to demand that we exalt him as God, reject him as a fraud of monstrous proportions, or believe him to be deeply disturbed. The middle ground is difficult to maintain.

Your friend,
Gene

SOUNDINGS

1. Have you met anyone who believed that Jesus was an evil man? Why do you suppose so many unbelievers refuse to categorize Jesus as evil or a fraud?

2. Have you ever met anyone who believed Jesus was a great moral teacher and a holy man but did not believe he was deity?

3. What evidence makes the claim improbable that Jesus was insane?

WAS JESUS GOD?

Chartings

Facts vs.
Theories

Resurrection

Prophecies

Miracles

November 23

Dear Lisa,

It was wonderful to hear that you believe your mother is getting better. Has she seen a doctor about her condition?

Yes, I agree with you; most people would probably be amazed to learn Jesus was mentioned in so many first- and second-century documents. I can send you additional historical references to the life of Jesus if you would like to see them.

You are right, of course, when you note that proving Jesus actually lived is a long way from proving he was divine. But we had to start somewhere.

Now you ask a good question: "How can you prove Jesus was God?" The answer to that question really depends on what you mean by proof. If your definition of proof requires that Jesus be produced before your very eyes, then I'm afraid I have no answer. But then, with that criterion of proof, it would be impossible to have confidence in the truthfulness of any historical event. How could you know George Washington was really the first President of the United States, if you refuse to believe anything you haven't personally witnessed? We believe George Washington was the first President because there is enough testimonial evidence to warrant the belief. Many of his contemporaries wrote about his presidency. We have various documents describing his presidency. Based on these evidences we believe George Washington was our first President. Dare I say we believe it by faith?

The reasons we are given as to why we ought to believe Jesus was divine are: (1) the miracles he performed (John 5:36), (2) the prophecies he fulfilled (John 5:39), and (3) his resurrection from the dead (1 Corinthians 15). The resurrection stands as the greatest proof of all, and it was the centerpiece of the first-century Christian message. And there is a good reason the resurrection played such a prominent role in the teaching of early Christians. As they understood it, the resurrection was a historical event capable of being proved beyond any reasonable doubt.

Lisa, none of these reasons listed above for accepting the deity of Jesus have anything to do with the ideas he espoused. That really is one of the things unique to Christianity. There were many great moral teachers before Jesus, and several came after him as well. But they are all dead. Only of Jesus is it claimed he rose from the dead. So the truthfulness of Christianity is not merely based on the things Jesus taught, but also on the historical fact of his resurrection.

As you consider the truthfulness of Christianity, you are being asked to consider whether or not Jesus was God in the flesh. The acceptance or rejection of what he taught is really secondary to who he was. If he was deity, then acceptance of what he taught naturally follows. If he weren't divine, then there is no reason to accept what he taught. We aren't talking about ideas to be received, but facts to be believed. Either Jesus worked the miracles that Matthew, Mark, Luke, and John said he did, or he didn't. Either Jesus was the fulfillment of prophecy, or he wasn't. Either Jesus rose from the dead, or he didn't.

Facts are not things to be argued with. We may debate theories and we may argue about what the facts imply, but the facts must be believed or rejected. With regard to the deity of Jesus, evidence for the miracles, prophecy, and the resurrection of Jesus must be considered. Then you must decide if they have enough credibility to be believed. And the body of evidence you must examine are the Gospel accounts of the life of Jesus, as presented by his contemporaries: Matthew, Mark, Luke, and John.

In a sense it is the writers themselves you are judging. Are Matthew, Mark, Luke, and John credible? Is there something about their writings that makes you believe they were making up the whole thing? Or maybe they weren't bad men, just deluded. Was Jesus just a slick teacher who managed to convince these people he was God? Is it possible they gave accurate accounts of the things they witnessed? Is it possible they were in their right minds when they wrote? Those are all matters for you to decide.

May God bless you in your quest.

Your friend,
Gene

SOUNDINGS

1. If Jesus was God in the flesh, how can it be necessary to examine his teachings in order to learn whether or not we should believe them?

2. Can one consistently believe Jesus is the Son of God but not accept some of his teaching? Why?

3. If Jesus was raised from the dead, how is it possible to consistently reject his deity?

Is There Sufficient Evidence for Jesus' Deity?

Chartings

- Credible Testimony
- Three Eyewitnesses
- Paul's About-Face
- Reasons for Rejection
- Dying for Beliefs

November 28

Dear Lisa,

Your last letter left my head spinning. I am certain I will not be able to reply to all of your questions. A theme that presented itself several times in your note was time. If I understand you correctly, you are concerned as to whether or not we can really place much confidence in our knowledge of events that happened so long ago. I understand your concern.

This is really a question about the nature of proof with regard to historical events. I can see I was less than convincing on this subject in my last letter, so let's have a go at it once more. Since we've already used George Washington as an example, let's stick with him. Most of us believe George Washington was a General in the Revolutionary War, crossed the Delaware River in a boat in the dead of winter, and went on to become the first President of the United States. Not only do we believe these things, but it has probably never crossed our minds to doubt them. We might even go so far as to say these are facts. And we would think someone quite odd who said he did not believe George Washington did the things I've mentioned.

That we accept these matters as facts shows we are not necessarily opposed to believing something to be factual even though we did not personally witness it. Not only have we never met George Washington, we haven't even talked to anyone who has met him or witnessed any of the events in his life. Still we believe. But why do we believe? Quite simply, because the testimony of those who did witness the events is credible.

There is a temptation to say there is a greater body of evidence about the life of George Washington than there is about Jesus'; therefore, belief in events about Washington's life has greater credibility than those about Jesus' life. Of course, one would expect a greater volume of evidence about an event that took place around 200 years ago, as opposed to one that occurred 2000 years ago. But the real issue is not the *amount* of evidence, but is the evidence *sufficient* to sustain the point in question. If the witnesses we have to the life of Jesus are credible, and if they capably testify to his actions, including the miracles, would their testimony be more true if we had more witnesses? If their witness is true, then it is true.

The discrepancy in the number of witnesses may not be as great as we imagine. How many people actually *saw* George cross the Delaware? Paul said that on one occasion Jesus appeared to over 500 people after the resurrection (1 Corinthians 15). Do you think the number of people that actually witnessed the Delaware crossing was substantially greater than that?

My point is, there are many events we believe with all our heart, despite the fact that the truthfulness of the event actually comes down to only a few who said they saw it. What we generally do is examine their testimony, then ask ourselves if there are any good reasons for rejecting what the witnesses said. We might reject testimony if the witnesses are known to be liars or otherwise of poor character. There might be something in the circumstances of the time of the event that causes us to question the reliability of a witness. Otherwise we usually accept the testimony unless we simply don't want to accept it for personal reasons.

Three eyewitnesses to the life of Jesus have left behind written accounts of what they saw. Those witnesses are commonly called Matthew, Mark, and John. We also have one account written by a man who examined the witnesses (Luke). The foremost question you must ask, Lisa, is whether or not you believe these men told the truth about the things they said took place. If you reject their testimony, then you ought to have a good reason for doing so.

While we are examining the accounts of those who actually saw Jesus, we should not fail to consider Paul's testimony. Paul did not believe Jesus was the Son of God. In fact, Paul considered it his personal mission in life to eliminate Christianity. In an odd twist, he ended up being the most zealous defender and promoter of the Movement. How did this happen? The explanation Paul offers for his change of mind is that he saw the resurrected Jesus (Acts 9, 22, 26). So powerful was that encounter that he turned his back on his former life, surrendered his personal advancement among the Jewish religious leadership, and followed Jesus to his death. His is a compelling testimony.

Is there something you know about these men that brings their credibility into question? None of them got wealthy because of their testimony about Jesus. Actually it was just the opposite. They clung to their testimony when threatened with punishment and death. Unless they were insane, it doesn't seem reasonable for them to die for a fabrication.

So unless we are going to reject the truth of all events that occurred prior to our own ability to recall them, we ought to be willing to entertain the possibility that Matthew, Mark, Luke, and John have provided truthful accounts of the life of Jesus.

Your friend,
Gene

SOUNDINGS

1. If something is proved to be true by three eyewitnesses, does it become more true if there are ten eyewitnesses? Explain your answer.

2. If you learned that Matthew, Mark, Luke, John, and Paul had become wealthy as leaders of the Christian movement, would it cause you to question their testimony?

3. Do you believe George Washington was the first President of the United States? Why do you believe? (a) because you are an eyewitness (b) because of the testimony of others.

4

The Resurrection

ARE MIRACLES POSSIBLE?

Chartings

- Superstitions
- Integrity vs. Lies
- Virgin Birth
- Ignorance

December 3

Dear Lisa,

I had hoped to respond more quickly, but you know how things can get as the holidays draw near. My daughter played piano at a Christmas recital this week. Forgive my boast, but I thought she was among the best.

Now, let's talk about miracles. In your last letter you expressed reservations about believing in miracles. You even proposed that people of the first century were, perhaps, a bit superstitious or ignorant and mistook events with natural explanations for miracles. While your suggested explanation does preserve the integrity of the authors of the four Gospels, it also implies that they were mistaken. Am I taking your response further than you intended?

We are certainly better informed about the way the world works today than men were 2000 years ago. But it would be difficult to explain all of the miracles surrounding the life of Jesus with the idea that his contemporaries were ignorant. Simply put, they may not have had all of the knowledge we possess, but they weren't that ignorant.

Consider the virgin birth narrative (Matthew 1). Many people have trouble with this miracle, even some believers. A man of virtue was betrothed to a woman of virtue, or so he believed. Now Joseph was no fool; he knew how babies were made. That is why he was prepared to end the engagement when he learned Mary was pregnant. He drew the natural conclusion that she had been unfaithful. It never crossed his mind that Mary was a virgin pregnant by divine influence.

Joseph was not a vengeful man. He had no desire to embarrass the woman he was once prepared to marry. But neither did he intend to marry her. What prompted Joseph to change his mind and marry her anyway? Matthew says an angelic visitation explaining that Mary was still virtuous changed his mind (Matthew 1:18–25). This can't be mere superstition, for we have already seen that Joseph was really quite practical. It can't be ignorance, for he knew where babies come from.

I really hate to sound repetitious, but it always comes back to the same question: Were the four Gospel writers men of integrity or were they liars? We really cannot escape that question.

Lisa, I understand there is a part of us that says, "I'll believe in miracles when I see one." But do we really limit our knowledge only to the things our senses personally experience? Of course not. There are many things we accept as facts beyond dispute, although we have never experienced them. We accept them purely on the basis that someone said they were so. And we aren't always very picky about the credentials of those whose word we are accepting. How many times have you been reading a book or a magazine article and said to someone, "Hey, did you know such-and-such was true? It says so right here."

History is filled with explorers' descriptions of places, animals, and experiences, many almost too strange to believe. Yet their testimonies were later confirmed. Just because we haven't seen a miracle doesn't mean they haven't happened.

Actually, you already admit to the most difficult part of the whole scenario. You believe in a supernatural Being. To be sure, you aren't sure what to call this Being, but whether you call this

Being a Presence, a Higher Power, or "Something out there," it still amounts to something beyond "natural." If there is a supernatural Being, why is it so hard to believe in the possibility of supernatural events? In fact, I should think it would be the very thing you would expect. The really odd thing would be if he did nothing at all.

Your friend,
Gene

SOUNDINGS

1. Why is it contradictory to believe in God and deny miracles?

2. What is a miracle?

3. Imagine you are returning to civilization after having discovered the geysers and sulphur springs at Yellowstone National Park or the duck-billed platypus in Australia. How would you describe what you had seen? How do you think it might sound to others?

PROPHECY AS PROOF OF THE DEITY OF JESUS

Chartings

- **Prophecy Criteria**
- **Divine Influence**
- **Fulfilled By Jesus**
- **Current Trends**

December 9

Dear Lisa,

Several weeks ago I mentioned to you that one of the reasons we ought to accept the deity of Jesus is because he fulfilled prophecies made hundreds of years before his birth. Let's look at this idea.

Most of us realize that the ability of a person to predict future events is an indication of the presence of God. In other words, it would require someone like God to provide that kind of information.

Now before we start hailing someone a prophet of God, their prophecies have to meet certain conditions so we might know their predictions constituted genuine prophecies and not merely good guesses. For example, their predictions would need to be far enough in the future to ensure they weren't simply recognizing trends already in motion. This would also put the matter beyond the prophet's ability to influence the outcome. The predictions would also need to be specific enough to be recognized as an actual prediction of an event. A statement so broad as to refer to many events cannot be considered a prediction of a specific event.

Most of us already recognize and use these tests of prophecy. We realize modern psychics stay with statements general in nature because they are bound to be true in one way or another. "You will fall in love" is a "prediction" true of most of us—eventually. I could predict that the sun will rise in the eastern sky next Tuesday morning, and I would be correct, but no one would consider me a prophet.

The prophets predicted hundreds of years in advance where the anointed One would be born (Micah 5:2), the time in which he would be born (Daniel 2:44), and the family from which he would come (Genesis 12:1–3). They spoke of many things about his life, but they also said a great deal about his death (Isaiah 53). They predicted he would be put to death for crimes he had not committed. They foretold he would be executed alongside criminals. All of these predictions, and many more, were made about the Messiah, and Jesus fulfilled all of them. But what is important to notice is that the predictions were given in such a way as to ensure they would point to the Messiah in a trustworthy manner.

The final book of the Old Testament was written about 400 years before the birth of Jesus. Clearly the Old Testament authors of the prophecies of the Christ could not have influenced the events they were predicting, and they obviously weren't looking at trends current in their day. Also, their predictions specified places, names, and events so they could be undoubtedly recognized. They were true prophecies.

Isn't it possible for someone to read prophecy and then set out to fulfill it? Of course, but note that Jesus fulfilled prophecies beyond human control. No one can have a say as to where or into which family he will be born. So it simply wasn't possible for Jesus to be a Messianic pretender.

Lisa, I have no way of explaining these predictions except that they happened by divine influence. And if these predictions claim the one who fulfills them will himself be divine, then logic compels me to accept the deity of that individual. Jesus fulfilled the prophecies, so Christians accept his divinity.

My family and I will be going out of town for a few days over the Christmas holidays. I hope to write you again before we leave. I would like to address the resurrection in my next letter.

Your friend,
Gene

SOUNDINGS

1. Why would it be ridiculous for an imposter to set out to fulfill the prophecies about the Messiah?

2. Make a list of things the prophets predicted about the Christ.

3. Apply the criteria for true prophecy—for example, the prediction is far enough in the future so as not to be a good guess—to people who claim to predict the future today. In what ways do the modern claims of prophecy fail to measure up to true prophecy?

POSSIBLE EXPLANATIONS FOR THE EMPTY TOMB

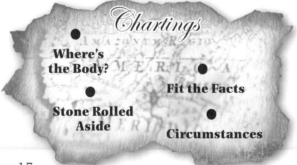

Chartings

Where's the Body?

Fit the Facts

Stone Rolled Aside

Circumstances

December 17

Dear Lisa,

We'll be leaving the day after tomorrow on a short skiing trip. I wasn't sure I would get around to writing this letter before we left, and I hope my rushing around will not diminish what I write.

Several weeks ago you asked why Christians believe Jesus was raised from the dead. I can't speak for all Christians, but for me the answer is quite simple: Given the circumstances of his death and entombment, the resurrection appears to be the explanation that best fits the facts.

Why don't we look at this as a kind of "who dun it?" I'll give you the facts as they are presented in the Gospel accounts, then you develop as many theories as you can to account for the facts. From there I'll leave it to you to accept the one you believe best explains the situation.

One Friday three men were crucified outside the city of Jerusalem. Two were convicted robbers. The third one was Jesus, who was apparently being executed as an enemy of the state. The next day was a Jewish holy day, so the request was made that the death of the criminals be hastened so they would not be hanging on the Sabbath, a violation of God's law. For this reason soldiers were sent to break the legs of the victims, which produced death by suffocation. They broke the legs of the robbers, but Jesus was already dead so he was left alone. His rapid death probably surprised the executioners since most victims of crucifixion lived much longer than six hours. One soldier confirmed Jesus' death by puncturing his side with a spear. Water and blood poured out of the wound. Apparently this separation of bodily fluids was taken as evidence that he was dead.

A wealthy disciple named Joseph asked the Roman governor for Jesus' body that it might receive a proper burial. Pilate consented and Joseph had Jesus' body placed in his personal tomb. The tomb was hewn out of the side of the mountain, so there was no rear entrance.

After placing Jesus' linen-wrapped body in the tomb, a large rock was rolled in place to block the entrance. A wax seal was also placed on the rock. Despite these measures, some feared the disciples might steal the body and claim Jesus had been raised from the dead. After all, Jesus himself had taught he would be raised after three days. For this reason Pilate also agreed to a request that soldiers be stationed outside the tomb.

On Sunday morning, Mary, one of Jesus' followers, returned to the tomb only to find the soldiers gone and the stone rolled aside. Mary spread the news and several other disciples went to the tomb. It must have seemed strange when investigation revealed that the only things left in the tomb were the linen wrappings; the body was gone.

Lisa, these are the facts presented by Matthew, Mark, Luke, and John. And now it is your turn. Put your wonderful mind to work and imagine various scenarios that would account for the empty tomb. Remember, the best explanation is the one that fits the facts. I look forward to reading what you come up with. You always have such a unique perspective.

I hope you have a great holiday season.

Your friend,
Gene

SOUNDINGS

1. What explanations have you heard to account for the empty tomb?

2. What explanation did the Jewish leaders give for Jesus' missing body? (See Matthew 28.)

3. How do the facts supporting the resurrection rule out other explanations for the empty tomb?

WHERE'S THE BODY?

January 4

Dear Lisa,

It sounds like you had a houseful of guests over the holidays. It was wonderful that your mother was able to be there for the celebration. I am sorry she is not improving as rapidly as you would like. Have you talked with the doctors about her progress? Maybe there is something they have overlooked.

I think you missed your life's calling. You should have been a detective. I can't conceive of any possible explanation for the empty tomb other than the ones you mentioned. So let's look at them.

You first propose the possibility that Jesus didn't really die on the cross. You offer the theory that perhaps he only passed out and was mistakenly thought to be dead. Such an idea would mean he lived out the remainder of his life in obscurity.

Did you know a movie was made some years back that set forth this very idea? The movie suggested Jesus survived the crucifixion and lived out his life in Rome. Various sects of the Muslim faith also teach that Jesus did not actually die on the cross, although they differ on the details of how he survived.

Here are some problems with this theory. The Roman soldiers reported that Jesus was dead, and they confirmed it by plunging a spear into his side. Various medical opinions have been offered through the years to explain the significance of the statement that not merely blood, but blood and water poured from the wound. Some medical experts believe the clear liquid was fluid built up around the lungs. I'm not a doctor so I'll leave such things to the experts, but this much is certain: that he was already dead was taken as positive proof by the soldiers assigned to hasten his death.

Even supposing he survived the cross and the spear to the side—not to mention the pre-crucifixion suffering (cf. Luke 22–23)—there is still the question of how he got out of the tomb. I can't imagine someone enduring what he had endured and then getting up, rolling away the stone, taking on the guards, and walking away. That would have been about as miraculous as the resurrection itself.

Another possibility you mention is that the disciples simply made up the whole thing. (Oh dear, so we are back to questioning the integrity of the disciples once again.)

Several matters come to mind. If the disciples had made up the resurrection story, the body would have been in the tomb. Why didn't the local authorities simply produce the body and end the entire charade? And if the body was missing, then who took it? Surely the local authorities didn't take it, else they would have ended the whole debate by producing the body. And the measures taken—guards and a seal—were for the purpose of making sure the disciples didn't steal the body. Besides, if what we have here is a case of grave robbers, doesn't it seem odd that they removed the linen wrappings and left them in the tomb? Grave robbers are usually in a hurry and aren't in the habit of undressing the corpse.

The disciples' story rings true and I'll tell you why: the Gospel writers agree that on the night Jesus was arrested they all ran away. Apparently only one of them was even present at the crucifixion. I find this interesting from what I know about human nature, especially men. People may admit to a number of faults, but the coward label is one we men usually refuse to accept. It seems pretty unbecoming, not to mention unmanly. But the disciples were willing to admit to cowardice. Why? I believe they accepted the charge for one simple reason: it was true. They were simply telling the facts. We have no record that they ever changed the story, even under the threat of a painful death. Almost any kind of conspiracy would have been broken under the pressure of such violence.

I am a Christian because I believe the resurrection best explains the facts surrounding the empty tomb. But I must admit you raised some intriguing possibilities.

Your friend,
Gene

P.S. Thanks for the invitation to the party you are having next week. Cindy and I are looking forward to seeing you and Blaine.

SOUNDINGS

1. What other explanations for the empty tomb were not addressed in this letter?

2. Have you ever asked an unbeliever to offer his explanation for the empty tomb? What did he say?

3. Would first-century Christians consider the resurrection a strong case for the truthfulness of Christianity? Why?

5

Does the Bible Contain Contradictions?

A PRINCIPLE FOR RECONCILING ALLEGED BIBLE CONTRADICTIONS

Chartings

- Reasonable Explanations
- Benefit of Doubt
- Investigate
- Reconcile

January 10

Dear Lisa,

There really is no need for you to feel bad about the negative re-marks made about religion and the Bible by one of the guests at your party. I could tell you were uncomfortable, undoubtedly on my be-half. I suspect we have all been unintentionally offensive at one time or another. If we look at the situation in just the right way, there is even a little humor involved. Maybe one day you can tell your friend that the fellow to whom he delivered his lecture on the failings of religion and the contradictions in the Bible is a preacher.

Your guest did raise a topic that you also have mentioned a time or two, though you introduced the matter with far greater finesse than your friend. Many people who reject the Bible cite alleged contradictions as the ground of their rejection. In fact, some have investigated the matter with great intensity and are quite capable of bringing up some rather puzzling situations in the Bible. Honest people with honest questions deserve honest answers.

Lisa, what I am going to say right now will probably surprise you, but I can't reconcile all of the alleged contradictions in the Bible with 100% assurance. Now please don't misunderstand me on this, for I'm not agreeing with your friend. He spoke as if he had 100% confidence in his conclusion that "the Bible is full of contradictions." (I believe that is how he put it.) I, on the other hand, have reconciliations to offer for the alleged contradictions, but I cannot be 100% sure my reconciliations are correct. Don't be fooled, the differences between these two positions are significant.

Here is an illustration of my position on alleged contradictions in the Bible. Suppose you are reading a letter from your mom. In the letter she sadly announces that her beloved dog died last week. But as she brings the letter to a close, she says she is going to take the dog for a walk. Now what is your initial reaction to this apparent conflict? Do you say to yourself, "Mom always was bad about lying"? Or is it possible your mom is losing her mind and is dragging the carcass of her beloved dog down the sidewalk? I doubt lying or lunacy would be your first consideration. Unless you have previous reasons for believing either of these conclusions, what you would probably do is go back and reread the part where you thought she said her dog died last week, looking for something that might explain what appears to be a contradiction. Are you being unreasonable? Of course not. You are simply giving your mother the benefit of the doubt. You have no reason to believe she would lie, and you don't think she is crazy, so you seek other explanations before you settle on the unpleasant ones. You might assume you misunderstood what you read. You may wonder if there is some bit of information that was left out. Perhaps mom got a new dog. But my point is, you look for and even assume there is an explanation for what you have read, even though you can't be sure of any of the possible reconciliations without further investigation.

My approach to the Bible is pretty much the way you would read a letter from your mom. Sure, it's possible mom is a liar or is crazy. But I must balance this horrible thought with the fact that she has been honest with me in the past and has always seemed quite level headed. Until the other alternatives appear unreasonable, why should I assume the worst rather than the best?

The Bible writers do not appear to have been mentally afflicted, and in the areas where it is possible to verify what they have written, they are shown to be honest. So why should I assume the worst, especially when there are reasonable explanations for what appears to be contradictions? The hardest part is deciding when a possible explanation becomes unreasonable.

Your friend,
Gene

SOUNDINGS

1. Have you ever challenged someone to point out some Bible contradictions? What was the outcome?

2. How does "giving the benefit of the doubt" mean more than just believing anything and everything presented to us without question?

3. Why should we "give the benefit of the doubt and seek a reconciling explanation" as a general practice—not only with the Bible?

WHAT IS A CONTRADICTION?

Chartings

● "Contradiction" Defined

● Witness Perspective

● Audience Perspective

● Confusions Cleared

January 16

Dear Lisa,

I am so glad your friend from the party also saw humor in the fact that he delivered a lecture on Bible contradictions to a preacher. I think a good sense of humor—especially when it comes to one's own slips—is essential to enjoying life. Who knows? Maybe one day he and I will get a chance to swap ideas about religion and the Bible.

It also seems your friend has some knowledge of the Bible from the questions he raised in your recent conversation with him. He is exactly right when he points out that all four Gospels mention the wording of the sign on Jesus' cross. He is also correct when he says none of the four accounts have the same wording for the sign. However, I do not believe, as your friend does, the differing accounts necessarily involve a contradiction.

I believe a lot of confusion regarding the Bible and alleged contradictions is cleared up by simply taking the time to give a precise definition as to what constitutes a contradiction. Here is a definition to ponder: statements are contradictory when it is impossible for both of them (or all of them) to be true at the same time.

It has been my experience that many so-called contradictions in the Bible are cleared up when we use the definition I have offered. But please be assured, I have not made up a special definition just to save the Bible embarrassment. If we would use this definition regularly we might find it can save us from making wrong personal judgments. It is all too common a mistake to assume because two accounts of something are different, then they must be contradictory. The truth is, unless the witnesses have conspired together, witnesses usually do differ in the way they present an event.

There are many reasons testimonies may differ in the accounts of an event. Perhaps the witnesses were standing in different places when the event took place. Maybe the purpose they have for telling the story is different, or the ones to whom they are telling the story differ in such a way as to cause them to emphasize certain details while omitting others. Sometimes people even use the same word in different ways, and what appears to be a contradiction is actually just a matter of semantics.

Let's use the party you had a few weeks ago as an example. How might different people describe your party? One guest might say it was a wonderful party, reporting that all the guests were really nice, well-mannered people and that your home was simply beautiful. That guest might comment on the architecture of your home, your manicured lawn, or the wonderful painting in the living room.

Another person might say that was one of the most boring parties he had ever attended. He might not even mention the condition of your home or that you have works of art on the walls. And just to make things interesting, suppose a third person says that was the wildest party she had ever attended. She might tell about guests shouting, loud music playing, and the trashed condition of the house.

Is it possible for all of these stories to be true? Can we account for the differences in these stories without resorting to some really outlandish interpretation? I believe we can. Some differences in the accounts are matters of personal taste. What constitutes a good or bad, boring or exciting party often depends on how the one telling the story defines a good time. Details about the artwork hanging on the walls may be omitted or mentioned depending on whether or not the one telling the story is into art (or believes those to whom he is conveying the story are interested in art). And even the differences regarding whether the party was wild or calm may depend on when the one telling the story left the party. Maybe the person reporting a calm party left before the guests relaxed. The point is, different does not necessarily mean contradictory.

The four Gospels do differ in their presentation of the life of Jesus, but that does not mean they are contradictory. Many of the differences are undoubtedly due to the audience the writer had in mind. Matthew might mention a detail he believes to be of particular importance to his readers, while the other writers may not mention it at all. They may even place events in different sequences depending on whether or not chronology is really important to their purpose.

Lisa, if you haven't done so, why don't you read the accounts of the crucifixion and see if there is something about the sign on the cross that makes it impossible for them all to be true? I am interested in the conclusions you draw about the wording of the sign on the cross.

Your friend,
Gene

SOUNDINGS

1. Examine the biblical accounts of the sign on Jesus' cross (Matthew 27:37; Mark 15:26; Luke 23:38; John 19:19). How do you reconcile the differences in the accounts?

2. Recall an occurrence that had two accounts that differed but were not contradictory. Why did the reports differ?

3. Discuss the strengths and weaknesses of the following definition of a contradiction: Statements are contradictory when it is impossible for all of them to be true at the same time.

A CONTRADICTION RECONCILED

Chartings

Common
Practice

Four Renditions

Jesus'
Enemies' Ire

Trilingual Text

January 20

Dear Lisa,

I am glad to hear Blaine is finally getting over that flu bug. Your remark is a common complaint among women: Men, and especially husbands, make lousy patients. Perhaps it is true that men are just "big babies" when we get sick.

Now, about the sign over the cross: The common practice of the Romans was to affix a sign above the head of the one being executed. The sign specified who was being executed and for what crimes he had been condemned. Jesus' sign was a bit strange since Pilate, according to the Gospel accounts, found no reason to condemn him. According to Matthew's account, Pilate, in the presence of Jesus' accusers, washed his hands, symbolizing his personal innocence in Jesus' execution. When you have found no real violation of the law, what do you have written on such a sign? Pilate perhaps took the opportunity to put one over on those he felt had forced him to condemn an innocent man. All four Gospel accounts say the sign said Jesus was "The King of the Jews." These words were, I suspect, intentionally chosen to irritate those who had called for Jesus' death.

The Gospel accounts have four renditions of the wording of the sign over the cross.

Matthew: THIS IS JESUS THE KING OF THE JEWS
Mark: THE KING OF THE JEWS
Luke: THIS IS THE KING OF THE JEWS
John: JESUS OF NAZARETH, THE KING OF THE JEWS.

I thank you for reading the biblical accounts and offering your judgment on any possible reconciliations of the differences. You are right when you say even though the differences are not major, still they are different and that needs to be explained. One possibility you offer is that Matthew, Mark, and Luke recorded abbreviations of what the sign said, while John gives the most complete account of the message. Such a possibility would mean their emphasis was on the statement "KING OF THE JEWS." I think there is much to this possible explanation. When we read John's account it is clear that the claim Jesus was the "King of the Jews" was the part that raised the ire of Jesus' enemies. After stating what the sign said, John gives the reaction of the chief priests. They asked Pilate not to write, "I am King of the Jews," but "he said, 'I am King of the Jews.'" Judging by the reaction some had to the sign, Matthew, Mark, and Luke provided that portion of the message their readers would consider most important.

The second possibility you offer is that some of them just got it wrong. That is not exactly the kind of thing I was hoping for. Still, you are right; it is a possibility.

After reading your letter I went back and read the accounts again. John's account intrigued me the most for two reasons. His is the one that generates most of the questions because his is the one that is most different. Mark and Luke are practically identical, and Matthew's addition is so slight I am not sure it would have raised any questions at all. A second reason John's account is of special interest is the fact that he was the only one of the four writers actually at the crucifixion. Being the only eyewitness may in itself explain the greater detail of his account.

However, as I read the accounts again, another possibility occurred to me. John mentions a detail easily overlooked when he states that the sign was trilingual, having been written in Hebrew, Greek, and Latin. This opens up a number of possibilities. Since the sign was written in three different languages, giving an exact quote of what it said is a little difficult. Most languages do not easily transfer directly into others without making certain modifications, which often involves simply giving the gist of what was written. It is also possible that only one of the languages contained the entire phrase given by John. It is not difficult to imagine Pilate using the Hebrew portion of the sign as a personal tool of vengeance to send a special message to the Jewish leaders.

The entire question of the message on the cross illustrates something I mentioned to you in our earlier correspondence. It is not always possible to provide a reconciliation that you know with 100% certainty is the solution to the situation. But I believe the solutions you and I have suggested are certainly possible, and none of these suggestions require us to stretch credibility. It is not necessary to charge the Bible with having a contradiction when there are so many other possibilities.

I hope Blaine quickly recovers from the flu. Meanwhile, I know you will do your best imitation of a no-nonsense nurse.

Your friend,
Gene

SOUNDINGS

1. Which, if any, of the possible reconciliations offered in this chapter appeal to you? Discuss other possible reconciliations.

2. Discuss the statement, "I have reconciliations to offer for the alleged contradictions, but I cannot be a hundred percent sure my reconciliations are correct."

3. Are most people likely to see the differences regarding the sign on Jesus' cross as contradictions that discredit the Bible, or does it seem that some people are merely looking for contradictions?

6

Christians Believe the Bible Is the Word of God

IS THE BIBLE FROM GOD?

Chartings

- Temple Prophecy
- False Claims
- Past Kingdoms
- Bible Survival

January 28

Dear Lisa,

First a preacher backs into your car in a parking lot, and now religious zealots come to your door. I suppose no one can blame you for wondering if God is "out to get you." Of course, another possibility is that you are becoming paranoid.

I'm just kidding. Let me assure you of this: when I backed into you a few months ago it was not a strange new evangelistic technique, though it is something to think about. But I doubt my insurance company would approve.

Yes, I have read the book your recent visitors brought to your door. As to whether or not you should read it is a matter for you to decide. I can say, as one who has read both it and the Bible, that reading one only served to increase my confidence in the other.

Since there are several books that claim to be revelations of the will of God, what is unique about the Bible? That is a good question.

If a book claims to be a revelation from God, there ought to be something about it that cannot be explained by mere human ingenuity. There are a couple of things about the Bible that appear to be beyond human capability. The most important is prophecy. You and I have already corresponded a bit on prophecy-related matters, so I'll not go over ground we've already covered about what constitutes a true prophecy. However, let's notice a couple of examples of fulfilled prophecy.

Some have the notion that God's prophets just sat around telling the future. Actually, most of them addressed the spiritual issues and behavior of people of their own day. But sometimes in these messages they spoke of things that had not yet happened. Their predictions were not for the purpose of satisfying our natural curiosity about what life would be like in the future, so they didn't address inventions and technology. Their concern was about morality and godliness. Most often their prophecies centered on the idea that immorality has consequences that may not be seen for many years, even centuries. And while their messages often spoke of future chastening for the misconduct of their readers, they usually concluded with hope beyond the chastisement.

King Solomon reigned over Israel's golden age. He presided over the erection of an elaborate temple, which he dedicated to Jehovah. But God's prophets predicted that a kingdom from the north would invade them, plunder and destroy the temple, take their wealth, and make captives of much of the population (Isaiah 39). This is precisely what happened around 586 B.C. when Nebuchadnezzar, king of Babylon, devastated Jerusalem. Interestingly enough, Isaiah, who lived in the latter half of the eighth century B.C., predicted that a king named Cyrus would give orders for the temple to be rebuilt (Isaiah 44:28). Babylon was not the major world power in Isaiah's day, and neither Nebuchadnezzar nor Cyrus had even been born. Isaiah predicted the rebuilding of a temple that wouldn't be destroyed for another 150 years; he gave the name of the king who would give orders for it to be rebuilt. I can't explain this without resorting to supernatural guidance.

Three of the four Gospels contain Jesus' prediction of the destruction of the temple. He predicted that his own generation would not pass away until the events of which he spoke were fulfilled. Jesus predicted the city would be surrounded by an embankment to prevent any citizens from leaving. He concluded by saying they will "level you and your children within you, to the ground; and they will not leave in you one stone upon another" (Luke 19:43–44). The temple was destroyed about 40 years later. The eyewitness account of the destruction written by the Jewish historian Josephus, who was not a Christian, stands as a great testimony to the accuracy of Jesus' prediction.

Lisa, I have no explanation for these predictions that does not involve the supernatural, and these prophecies are one of the reasons I believe the Bible is from God.

If you stop and think about it, even the Bible's existence is difficult to explain apart from divine intervention. Roman authorities tried to destroy the Christian writings. Some Christians were tortured in attempts to learn where they kept their books. Yet the Bible survived. Is this merely an amazing coincidence or a sign of divine favor?

Your friend,
Gene

SOUNDINGS

1. The Bible is not the only book that claims to be from God. Why do we believe the Bible is inspired of God and the other books are not?

2. What are your favorite biblical prophecies? Why?

3. How might one explain fulfilled prophecy while rejecting the divine inspiration of the Bible?

SUPERSTITION AND THE BIBLE

Chartings

Paths in
the Sea

Inspiration

Knowledge vs.
Enlightenment

Cutting Edge
Health Codes

Biblical
Scientific Insight

February 3

Dear Lisa,

I am sorry it took me a little longer than usual to reply to your last letter. Last week is one of those weeks I am glad to have behind me. In midst of all of the chaos, I thought about your comment concerning whether God was out to get you. I wondered if his counterpart was out to get me.

Anyway, about superstition and the Bible. Yes, I have heard the charge made a time or two that the Bible is merely a book full of ancient superstitions. I believe it is a difficult subject to discuss, since almost all those of every culture and every generation believe they are more enlightened than their predecessors. But being more knowledgeable is not the same as being more enlightened. Surely our knowledge base grows as each generation builds on the accomplishments of its predecessors, but that knowledge doesn't always translate into superior moral and ethical views and behavior. Nevertheless, a couple of generations from now our great grandchildren will be looking back on us as if we were the Flintstones.

The Bible contains a lot of information well ahead of its time. Matthew Fontaine Maury is not exactly a household name. But there are a lot of sailors who are glad he came along. Maury, confined to bed with an illness, asked his son to read to him from the Bible. His son chose to read Psalm 8, which says God has dominion over "the birds of the air, and the fish of the sea that pass through the paths of the seas" (Psalm 8:8). The phrase, "the paths of the seas," caught Maury's attention, and he determined that if the Bible says there are paths in the seas he would find them. He made a study of wind and currents from ship's logs and discovered that the seas are circulating. He charted sea lanes and currents, and wrote one of the early textbooks of oceanography: *Physical Geography of the Sea.* An account of Maury's discovery is given in *Matthew Fontaine Maury: Pathfinder of the Seas,* published by the U.S. Naval Institute in 1927. But my point is, the psalmist was referring to the paths of the seas long before men knew of them.

Israel was certainly not backward in her health code. Sanitation laws in Leviticus and Deuteronomy forbade human waste within the camp and called for its burial (Deuteronomy 23:12–13). Israel was not allowed to eat animals that had died from natural causes. Strict quarantine laws kept disease from spreading (Leviticus 13–14). Many supposedly advanced societies have ignored these laws and suffered greatly in the process.

One of the more interesting statements in this area was made by Isaiah in the eighth century B.C. He spoke of God as "He who sits above the circle of the earth" (Isaiah 40:22). We do have record that four or five centuries later some Greek philosophers advanced the notion that the earth is not flat. But we all know the story of Christopher Columbus' voyage in A.D. 1492, which conclusively proved the earth was round. Isaiah's statement seems to have been well ahead of its time. The Old Testament book of Job even appears to mention dinosaurs (Job 40:15–24).

Lisa, many scholars have found an amazing number of biblical statements that appear to be well ahead of their day. These kinds of statements indicate two things to me. First, the oft spoken idea that the Bible is a book full of ancient superstitions is not as easily sustained as some allege. The second matter indicated, I will put in the form of a question: Where did the Bible writers get their information? Were they simply lucky guesses? Since these kinds of statements were beyond human knowledge of their day, I believe the writers were directed by God, a process commonly called *inspiration.*

What do you think?

Your friend,
Gene

SOUNDINGS

1. List other instances in which the Bible reveals information ahead of its time.

2. Explain how you would feel if you were to make a scientific discovery based on a biblical statement.

3. Discuss the subject of faith in the context of Matthew Fontaine Maury's determination that if the Bible says there are paths in the sea he would find them.

DOES THE NEW TESTAMENT CONTAIN HUMAN OPINION?

Chartings

Promised Guidance

Writer's Opinion?

Answers from God

Discretion

February 8

Dear Lisa,

Your theory is interesting. I can also see how something like what you suggest could easily happen if one were not very careful. I think you are correct in your thought that inspiration was not a full-time gift. I'm sure Paul wrote a number of things that were not inspired. If Paul ever wrote a grocery list, to use your rather quaint example, he certainly was not divinely guided.

The guidance Jesus promised his apostles had to do with their function as witnesses to the resurrection and as teachers of God's will. This seems pretty clear from Matthew 10:19–20: "But when they deliver you up, do not worry about how or what you should speak. For it will be given to you in that hour what you should speak; for it is not you who speak, but the Spirit of your Father who speaks in you." Clearly, Jesus was not promising divine guidance in every aspect of their lives.

Is it possible, then, that the inspired documents might contain sections that were the writer's personal judgment? Yes, I think you have hit on more than merely a possibility, I believe it actually happened.

It is your last question that I find disturbing and frightening. You ask: "What would happen if the writers did not always carefully distinguish between inspired commands and personal judgments?" I assume what you are getting at is the possibility of a writer's giving God's will, then moving to his personal opinion without mentioning the change. The writer's opinion would be characterized as divine will. Your question "What would happen?" can be answered in one word: chaos! Bible study would be a nightmare for all of us if we had to try to separate divine injunctions from personal judgments without help from the author.

Fortunately, we have an example. In 1 Corinthians 7, Paul is discussing several aspects of marriage. In verse 10, he states: "Now to the married I command, yet not I but the Lord: A wife is not to depart from her husband." But when we read a little further Paul addresses a different aspect of marriage with these words: "Now concerning virgins: I have no commandment from the Lord; yet I give judgment as one whom the Lord in His mercy has made trustworthy" (1 Corinthians 7:25).

In verse 10 he had been asked whether a married person ought to remain married. He states clearly that the answer he was about to give was from the Lord. In verse 25 he was asked whether an unmarried person should marry. He recommended staying single because of an unusual circumstance, which he calls "the present distress" (7:26). But, he plainly states that this is not a command from God but a personal recommendation. Clearly the information he gave from the Lord was viewed as something all men were obligated to accept, while his opinion was a matter of option.

Please don't misunderstand me on this point. When Paul gave his opinion, I believe he did so by means of divine guidance. Inspiration allowed Paul to offer his opinion, and in couching it as Paul's advice the readers are told God places them under no obligation to marry or refrain from marrying. It is a matter left up to the discretion of the individual.

From this I conclude that the New Testament writers were quite careful to distinguish between their personal opinion and a revelation from God.

In addition to the writers' claims, I believe it is also valid to point out that a God wise enough to create us is surely capable of communicating his will clearly. I should hate to think God suffers from poor communication skills.

Your friend,
Gene

SOUNDINGS

1. Why does it surprise students that the Bible contains a man's opinion?

2. Are there other areas of our lives, like the one mentioned in 1 Corinthians 7:25, where God has left us free to do what we think is best?

3. Discuss the phrase "the present distress." Do circumstances ever become a part of important decisions we must make? If so, does that mean we are practicing situation ethics?

WHY BIBLES READ DIFFERENTLY

Chartings

- Hebrew and Greek
- Language Changes
- Ancient Manuscripts
- Authenticity

February 15

Dear Lisa,

Happy Birthday!

It sounds like a very nice Bible your mom gave you for your birthday. The fact that it doesn't read exactly like your old Bible should be no cause for alarm. That really is easily explained.

The Bible was not originally written in English. The Old Testament was written in Hebrew, with a few portions of Aramaic, a language related to Hebrew. The New Testament was written in Greek. So both your old Bible and your new Bible were translated from these languages into English. The reason your new Bible and your old one do not read exactly alike is because they are two different translations. Remember that in your high school foreign language course, different students translated the same sentence in different ways, none of them necessarily wrong. The same is true for translations of the Bible.

There are a couple of reasons new Bible translations are being produced. All living languages change, and English is no exception. A translation might be so old that it no longer reflects the way modern readers write and speak, in which case the translation loses some of its effectiveness in communicating the biblical message. New translations do not become necessary only because of the changes in modern English, but also because our knowledge of the ancient Hebrew and Greek languages continues to expand through archaeological finds. Sometimes we learn that a certain word car-d a slightly different meaning from what we previously thought. This knowledge enables us to improve our translations.

But there is another reason that new translations may become important, and this reason relates to something you asked me about a couple of weeks ago. You asked whether or not we can really know that the Bible we have accurately reflects the work of the original writers.

The Bible undoubtedly has better manuscript attestation than any other ancient book. This is really quite amazing when you consider how many attempts have been made to rid the world of the Bible. Some early Christians were willing to die rather than surrender copies of the New Testament writings to hostile Roman authority. And while it is true we do not have the original documents of the New Testament, we have portions that date from the second century. Most of these copies are fragmentary, while a few are complete or near complete copies of the entire New Testament. There are thousands of these manuscripts, and by studying and comparing them we can approach the Bible with confidence that it truly reflects the original writings.

How these ancient manuscripts were discovered is an interesting study. Many very old manuscripts of New Testament documents were discovered in ancient churches, monasteries, and synagogues. But the most famous discovery was made shortly after World War II. A shepherd boy, searching for one of his animals, threw a rock into a cave near the Dead Sea. A shattering sound aroused his curiosity. He discovered the first of 11 caves containing the library of a Jewish sect that predated Jesus himself. Some of these Hebrew manuscripts date nearly to the fourth century B.C. These caves contained Hebrew manuscripts of all or part of almost every book of the Old Testament.

There are two additional lines of evidence that give us confidence that what we have truly reflects the original biblical documents. Christianity spread so quickly throughout the ancient world that the Bible was soon being translated into many languages. We have copies of some of these ancient translations. They provide more evidence as to the wording of the original writings. Second, early Christians wrote many letters, religious essays, and books within which they quoted passages of Scripture. From those writings we learn how their ancient copies of the Bible read. Their work further validates the authenticity of our present-day Bibles.

The massive evidence that supports today's Bible as the word of God is quite impressive. The biggest challenge is not to determine if we have writings true to the original ones; rather, are we willing to examine what we have?

Your friend,
Gene

SOUNDINGS

1. How do the different translations available today benefit or harm the cause of Christ?

2. Are all translations equal, or are some better than others? What are the characteristics of a good translation?

3. How do you determine which translations are the best?

7

Human Suffering

WHY DO GOOD PEOPLE SUFFER?

Chartings

- **No Satisfaction**
- **Wickedness**
- **Job's Demands**
- **Trusting God**

February 20

Dear Lisa,

I am so sorry. I know you had high hopes your mother's illness was behind her. I am sure it was a terrible shock to learn of her cancer. The prognosis does not sound encouraging. Two months is not a very long time and I am sure a doctor would not make such a prediction without feeling rather confident about the information.

Your question is understandable under the circumstances. The question of why bad things happen to good people has been discussed through the ages, seemingly with no satisfactory resolution.

The question of human suffering usually carries with it two problems that make it difficult to answer. The first problem is that we usually ask the question at a time when we are least prepared to deal with it. It is not easy to be calm and rational about our own illness or the illness of a loved one.

But there is a greater problem our personal tragedy brings to this question. When someone we love is suffering, a perfectly logical answer as to why there is human suffering will not satisfy most of us. More than anything, we want the illness to go away. We want to feel better. I am afraid I can offer no answer that will take away your pain. I'm sorry.

The most extensive treatment on the subject of human suffering in the Bible is the book of Job. Job was a wealthy man who in a short span of time lost his wealth, his children, and finally his health. Most of the book consists of a discussion between Job and three of his friends. Job's friends insist he must be guilty of great wickedness to be suffering so intensely. They tell him if he will simply repent he might get better. But Job maintains his innocence, and rightfully so. The book concludes with God himself entering the discussion as he chastises Job's friends for their unfounded accusations against Job's character.

In his frustration Job had demanded several times that God show himself and explain why all the bad things had happened to him. So after dealing with Job's friends, God turns his attention to Job himself and the arrogant challenges he had made. God asks Job a series of questions about the universe that are beyond Job's ability to answer. In asking these questions God is, quite frankly, revealing to Job his own ignorance. If Job cannot comprehend these matters about God's creation, then what makes him think he is in a position to judge the way God is running things?

Biblical answers to human suffering are not what most of us want to hear. We want to know why, and God's answer is that we ought to trust his wisdom. Any answer that requires trust is going to be difficult to accept.

Though the biblical response to the question of human suffering falls short of our expectations, it does remove the misguided notion that we suffer in direct proportion to our sins. Just because someone is suffering doesn't mean he is evil. I suppose this does provide some comfort.

As for your confusion over why your mother seems to be handling all of the bad news better than you, I think that is a question you ought to ask her. She has a perspective on these things that none of us can comprehend. You have spoken of her faith often. You describe her as a brave lady, so why don't you talk to her?

And you need not feel funny about asking me to pray for your mother. It is not necessary for you to understand why you asked; it is sufficient that you did ask.

Your friend,
Gene

SOUNDINGS

1. Do people always suffer in direct proportion to the sin in their lives? How did those in Jesus' day associate sin and suffering? (John 9:1–2).

2. What are some aspects of human suffering that are beyond the understanding of most of us?

3. Did Job come to understand why he was suffering? What can we learn from this fact?

HOW CHRISTIANS FACE SUFFERING

Chartings

- Ultimate Destination
- Preparation
- Life's Legacy
- Optimism

February 28

Dear Lisa,

I am glad you had an opportunity to talk with your mother about her illness, as well as her seemingly incomprehensible optimism. As you noted, it is not an unrealistic hope of a cure that is sustaining her spirits. She is optimistic because she believes that even if she is not cured she is going to a better place. The biblical basis for believing there is a better place is founded on the promises of Jesus, as well as the testimony of others who claim to have seen that place either personally or in a vision (John 14:2–3; 2 Corinthians 12:2–4; Revelation 21:22).

I understand your concern that living for another world would seem to lead to a lack of appreciation and care for this world. Here is a helpful analogy.

The Christian view of life is like that of a man who sets out on a trip from New York to California. The traveler sees many alluring sights along the way. Some are so lovely he is tempted to linger. He even changes his plans and stays longer than he planned at certain stops. But despite how enraptured he becomes with things along the way, he continues to move toward his ultimate destination. He is always sad to leave behind newly discovered treasures, but he looks forward to discovering new and even better sights.

Christians see this life very much like the trip I just described. Heaven is our ultimate destination, but we still enjoy the trip. We encounter many meaningful things along the way that make us want to stay. Love for our mate, children, family, and friends makes life so wonderful that the thought of leaving is sad. But once it is clear we are leaving, we may then turn our attention to our real destination.

Seeing this world as a temporary stop on a longer journey does not have to mean being less concerned or less active in life's affairs. Christians desire to conduct themselves in such way that others will say the world is a better place for their having been here. As Christians we desire to alleviate human suffering as we are able, and we hope to leave behind a planet fit to be enjoyed by others. However, when it is time to leave, we look forward to something even better at the end of the journey.

Your mom's attitude toward her illness is just what one might expect. She has enjoyed the lovely things this life has to offer, and now she is prepared to move on.

My prayers continue to be with you.

Your friend,
Gene

SOUNDINGS

1. What is a pilgrim? (1 Peter 1:1; 2:11; Hebrews 11:13). How does the pilgrim concept relate to the Christian view of life on earth?

2. What are some of the things that cause Christians to forget this life is only temporary?

3. What can we do to remind ourselves this world is only a temporary stop on an eternal journey?

CAN GOD PREVENT ALL SUFFERING?

Chartings

Rules of
the Universe

Paul's
Thorn

Selective
Healing?

Freedom's
Abuses

Spiritual
Purpose

March 6

Dear Lisa,

I am glad you see the beauty in the way your mom is facing her situation. It is also understandable that you wonder why a good and all-powerful God allows anyone to suffer. Many great minds have set themselves to answer that question, so I am under no delusion it can be easily handled. Here is my understanding of the matter.

As I read your letter it occurred to me that you were really asking two questions. First you wanted to know why God even allows suffering at all since he is supposed to be all-powerful and omnibenevolent. Second, you wondered why God doesn't simply heal people when they get sick. You even hinted that perhaps he is not as powerful as we imagine.

Lisa, I don't believe the question is whether or not God can heal your mother or any other sick individual, for without a doubt he can. The Bible tells us that God has healed people with all kinds of diseases. We read of lame people walking, deaf people hearing, and the blind receiving their sight. Sometimes even the dead were raised. God has the power to heal diseases. However, even in the first century when miracles seemed so prevalent, not everyone was healed. Paul worked many miracles but he told Timothy to drink a little wine for his stomach's ailment. Later he wrote: "Trophimus I have left in Miletus sick" (1 Timothy 5:23; 2 Timothy 4:20). Paul himself admitted that he had a "thorn in the flesh" for which he prayed three times that it might be taken away, only to be told: "My grace is sufficient for you, for My strength is made perfect in weakness" (2 Corinthians 12:7–10). Why some people are healed and others are not is a mystery known only to God.

I think part of the problem is that we usually begin with the assumption that all suffering is bad, therefore if God were truly good he would end all suffering or not allow it in the first place. But is it proper to assume pain and suffering are always bad things? Paul said his suffering taught him humility (2 Corinthians 12:7). Even dying itself can be a way of sparing us unforeseen future horrors. "The righteous perishes, and no man takes it to heart; merciful men are taken away, while no one considers that the righteous is taken away from evil" (Isaiah 57:1).

Healthy or sick, life and death are very unpredictable situations in this life. The Bible admits that this is true; life is "a vapor that appears for a little time and then vanishes away" (James 4:13–17). It seems to me this fact accomplishes two things. It makes us aware of our own humanity. We humans have a way of forgetting that God is ultimately in control and not ourselves. There is much to be learned from the knowledge of our own frailties. Moses wrote: "So teach us to number our days, that we may gain a heart of wisdom" (Psalm 90:12).

The unpredictability of life also has a way of reminding us that one day we will stand before God in judgment (Hebrews 9:27). This unpredictability appears to be part of God's plan. Such should cause a thinking person to consider the importance of each day, knowing it may be the last.

As to why God allows suffering, it is helpful for us to look at the big picture rather than limiting ourselves to isolated cases. Suffering comes about in many different ways, and some of them are more easily understood and accepted than others. I also believe some have unreasonable expectations concerning what God ought to do about suffering.

God has chosen to make this universe operate on consistent principles. We often refer to these principles as Laws of Nature. Many times people suffer because they willingly choose to engage in practices that defy these rules of the universe. For example, very large grown men go out on a football field and collide with all of their might, yet no one is supposed to get hurt. People who decide to scale mountains for a hobby risk the inevitable reality that if they lose their grip they will fall to death or injury. Each sportsman enters these situations knowing the laws by which God's creation operates. When large moving objects collide, damage is done and things get broken. When you lose your grip on the mountain there is no sense in hoping gravity will cease. The laws that govern our universe are really a great blessing, as they allow us to predict the outcome of certain situations and act accordingly. But just as the outcome of events is predictable when we are operating in harmony with these laws, they are also predictable when we put ourselves in conflict with them.

Sometimes even when we avoid unnecessary risk, the poor decisions made by others affect us. When a drunken driver hits us or when a child brings a loaded gun to school, suffering is almost always the result. There is an enormous temptation on our part to say, "Surely God could have done things differently. There must be a better way." That is merely an assumption. Such thoughts bring us back to the book of Job once again. Job complained about the way God handles the affairs of this life until God made him realize he really didn't know enough about running a universe to question his methods (Job 38–42).

We sometimes erroneously assume God can do anything. Some things cannot be done because they involve inner contradictions. God cannot make a round square, for example, because the very concept of a round square is a logical contradiction. If it is a square than it can't be round and nothing short of changing the very nature of what we mean by a square can make it possible to create a round square. I know this probably sounds like the kind of thing people with very little to do must sit around and think about, but there is a much more important application to this principle than squares and circles. Much suffering is brought about by those who exercise their God-given right to choose those things that can or will bring harm to themselves or others. Yet free will, the ability to make decisions, is one of the blessings we prize most highly. In fact, I feel certain should we be given the choice of no suffering through losing our ability to choose our own course, most would accept the possibility of suffering. However, freedom must be used wisely. One of the things even God cannot do is create a being with the ability to choose right or wrong, good or evil, while at the same time making it impossible for that being to make the wrong choice. Free will brings with it the possibility that someone will abuse it, which almost always leads to suffering.

We understand that people who choose to be sexually promiscuous often end up with diseases ranging from the inconvenient to the deadly. We understand that babies born to mothers who use drugs or alcohol often suffer due to mom's abuse. But in your mother's case there is no easily seen cause. She didn't smoke or involve herself in other high-risk behaviors. However, we must realize that just because we can't see the reason for suffering doesn't mean there isn't one. Perhaps the surge in the number of people getting cancer has something to do with things we have done to our environment or even our eating habits. The hard part is not knowing why.

Just as it is wrong to assume an all-powerful God can do anything, it may also be wrong to assume a good and loving God must eliminate all suffering. Physical pain is often very helpful. It causes us to remove our hand from the hot stove, preventing further burns. It causes us to give our leg the rest it needs for a sprained ankle to heal. It causes us to seek medical attention, and perhaps solve a minor health problem before it becomes major. And sometimes it is not even our own pain that causes us to seek medical attention or alter our lifestyle. When someone becomes ill it often causes people close to them to get a checkup or change unhealthy habits.

Just as pain has a beneficial physical function, it may very well be that pain and suffering have a spiritual purpose as well. It has been my own experience that those in the midst of tremendous joy or horrible crisis often begin to think about God. Status quo, on the other hand, seldom produces a contemplative mind.

The difficulty with seeing that suffering in some way helped to make us a better person is that we are rarely able to see it while we are in the midst of the situation. Many people look back on difficult times and see themselves as being a better person for it, but during a crisis our attention is more toward present relief than future maturity.

I am sorry I have no words to offer that will take away your pain. If in some way I may help you during this time of need, please call on me.

Your friend,
Gene

SOUNDINGS

1. What purpose might the unpredictability of life serve in helping us live in a way that pleases God?

2. Discuss the absurd idea of God's granting freedom of choice to those who do not have the ability to make bad choices.

3. What is the advantage of God's designing people who can serve Him by choice?

8

Christianity and Moral Issues

WHEN PERSONAL CONVICTIONS CLASH WITH THE BIBLE

Chartings

Roots of My Convictions

Bible Authority

Teach My Child

What to Trust

March 12

Dear Lisa,

These certainly must be confusing times for you. First there is the sadness of your mother's illness. Then, after several years of trying, you learn you are finally pregnant. I think the phrase you are looking for is "A time to be born and a time to die." Your mother's advice sounds very wise to me. You should not let her illness rob you of the joy of carrying your baby.

I can understand why you did not want to announce your pregnancy immediately. My wife was also a couple of months along before she wanted anyone to know she was expecting. Her fear was that should something tragic happen, the fewer people who knew, the better.

You are not the first woman who upon learning she was going to have a baby began viewing religion with renewed interest. The pending birth of a child has motivated more people, especially women, to examine their beliefs than any other single event. As you rightly observed, you need to come to grips with your own convictions, or your child is bound to grow up with the same awkward feeling of being somewhere in the middle regarding God. I also have been in that place, and it is not a very comfortable place to be. A woman once said to me: "It is one thing for me to ignore the subject of God; it is an entirely different matter for me to teach my child to ignore God."

I knew from the beginning that addressing your concerns about some of the moral views set forth in the Bible was inevitable. Several different situations will arise as we look at some of your questions. In some cases you will undoubtedly find the Bible really doesn't teach what you have been led to believe it teaches. These will be the easy situations where you will find you are in essential agreement with the biblical view. But I am under no delusions that it will always be that easy. There will be other situations where your long held convictions are in conflict with what the Bible teaches. At that point you will be once again forced to address an issue we have already discussed: Is the Bible really a revelation of the will of God, or is it simply an ancient religious book purely of human origin? You will also need to ask a couple of questions about your personal convictions. Most people never stop to ask simple questions like, where did my personal convictions come from? And why should I trust my convictions above the view taught by the Bible?

There is one final option to be considered. Sometimes when we try to learn what the Bible teaches about a matter, we find the subject is not directly addressed at all. Or sometimes the subject is left in the realm of personal preference. This becomes a very difficult area because most people, Christians and non-Christians alike, are seldom content to leave things up to the individual. We may agree that a certain view is a matter of personal preference, but we can't help but believe our personal preference is better than everybody else's. Of course, then we set out to convert everyone to our preference. In religion there is a real danger of elevating our personal preference to the status of a biblical mandate.

From previous conversations I already know some of your concerns. We might as well jump right in and start with the biggest one, so let me know what bothers you most.

Congratulations on your wonderful news.

Your friend,
Gene

SOUNDINGS

1. Where do most people learn their convictions regarding right and wrong?

2. Why is it best to first examine the biblical teaching of Jesus as the Son of God rather than opinions on moral issues?

3. How can we avoid forcing our opinions on others?

DOES THE BIBLE ENDORSE SLAVERY?

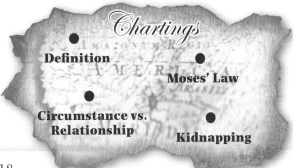

Chartings

- Definition
- Moses' Law
- Circumstance vs. Relationship
- Kidnapping

March 18

Dear Lisa,

I neglected to ask you when the baby is due. I am sure you and Blaine are making all kinds of plans for what you would like to accomplish before the baby gets here. You will most likely not have most of them done when the big day comes.

When you decide to start with issues, you start in a big way. The way the Bible deals with slavery has long been a point of discussion. Some have rejected the Bible because they believe it endorses slavery. Many have that notion because they are looking for a specific prohibition of the practice. In some cases the condemnation they are looking for is there, but the way it is addressed sometimes makes it difficult to make the connection.

First, let us define slavery. The Old Testament made provisions for people to indenture themselves in order to pay their debts. While I would not like to do that, it is certainly not immoral.

It seems that much of the slavery in the Old Testament was closely akin to what we call prisoners of war. What do you do with people you capture in times of war? As I see it you only have three choices: (1) You can allow them to assimilate into your society if they wish to do so, which the Law of Moses allowed; (2) you can kill them; or (3) you can make them serve you. A fourth alternative would be to simply turn them loose, but in the middle of a war that is not very practical.

Moses' law also made provisions for slaves to be released at an appointed time—the year of jubilee (Leviticus 25:8–55). In that year all slaves had to be released, unless they wished to remain servants.

When most Americans think of slavery, they envision slavery in early America—people captured, sold, and forced to work against their will. The Bible certainly condemns that practice, otherwise known as kidnapping (Deuteronomy 24:7). The Old Testament referred to it as "man-stealing." This biblical condemnation of slavery is often missed.

For many years I struggled with the New Testament concept of slavery. I wondered why there was no direct statement commanding the release of slaves. I have reached three conclusions on this subject.

First, we must remember that Jesus did not make a pronouncement on every specific social issue. Often he spoke in broad principles that we must apply to specific situations. If you think about it, that approach makes more sense for one who is setting forth teachings that will transcend one's specific culture and time. Jesus condemned slavery when he taught that the second greatest commandment was to "love your neighbor as yourself" (Matthew 22:39). Jesus' disciples repeated this teaching. In fact, one disciple takes it a step further when he adds, "Love does no harm to a neighbor; therefore love is the fulfillment of the law" (Romans 13:10). These are hardly the words of people who endorsed tearing people from their families, transporting them across the ocean, and selling them to the highest bidder.

Second, the New Testament law is not a civil and religious law; therefore, it does not address social issues in the form of what the government ought to do about them. The New Testament points out that civil government exists to punish evil and reward good (Romans 13:1–4), but neither Jesus nor his disciples taught civil rebellion. I believe many churches have exchanged their God-given mission for a political mandate. I do not think churches ought to try to run the state. That does not mean individuals within a church should not vote, but the church should not be confused with a political action committee. Christianity is not a battle for people's bodies, but for their minds. Our battles are those of ideas and a desire to win a person's heart, not to force them into subjection. The main effect Christianity has on the civil government is indirect through the changes it makes in the lives of individuals.

I have left for last a principle I believe to be most important because it involves the entire Christian perspective of life. The most important thing to a Christian is not his circumstances in this life but his relationship with God. Perhaps the best words I can find to describe this are in 1 Corinthians 7:21–24: "Were you called while a slave? Do not be concerned about it; but if you can be made free, rather use it. For he who is called in the Lord while a slave is the Lord's freedman. Likewise he who is called while free is Christ's slave. You were bought at a price; do not become slaves of men. Brethren, let each one remain with God in that state in which he was called."

The general teaching is this. If you can change your slave status, then by all means do so, but your status in life does not hinder or enhance your standing before God. That teaching must have been powerful in a society that considered slaves to be inferior. From the Christian perspective where one stands before God is paramount. I don't have to like my situation in life, but I have the assurance that the thing most important doesn't depend on whether I am a slave or free.

In short, in the New Testament the stress is not on social reform but on winning the hearts of individuals to God. From the Christian perspective, the most important thing is where I stand in the eyes of God, not society.

The Christian perspective teaches that injustices will always be present in this world. That doesn't mean we have to like them, just expect them. If this world were perfect, then I guess there would be no need for heaven. As it is, the rain falls on the good and the bad, and the sun shines on the just and on the unjust. The reason for this, I believe, is to create a situation where people choose to love and serve God because it is the right thing to do, and not merely for personal gain.

I know this letter has been rather long, but I did want to be thorough.

Your friend,
Gene

SOUNDINGS

1. When did Jesus or his followers ever give any laws to the civil government?

2. Discuss 1 Corinthians 7:21–24. How do you suppose slaves reacted to these words?

3. What is the job of Christians: to change civil laws or to bring people to salvation? Support your answer.

VIOLENCE IN THE BIBLE

Chartings

Facts, not Endorsement

Moral Battles

Destruction as Justice

Purpose

March 24

Dear Lisa,

Yes, there is a good deal of violence in the Old Testament, but I disagree with your comparing it to the violence one might see in a modern movie. The God-ordained wars and violence depicted in the Bible are not impulsive acts of madmen. God did not give instruction for the destruction of a nation on the basis of a lust for power or territory. God always has moral reasons for such destructions to be warranted.

Lisa, I dislike war. Movies often depict war with a vengeful hero coming through to save the day. Real war is brutal: people die or are physically and emotionally scarred. Our Veteran's Administration hospitals and clinics are proof of this. A soldier told me, "If you find someone who likes war, then you have found someone who has never been in one."

However, as ugly as war is, I think we would agree there are times when it would be wrong not to do battle. When Germany was slaughtering Jews by the millions and invading neighboring countries, it would have been immoral to simply watch. When God called upon one nation to go to war with another, the reason was always a moral one.

Sometimes people miss the moral issues behind the wars of the Old Testament because of the way the Bible is divided. The Old Testament has a section of books called the books of history. These books relate many acts of human cruelty. But it is not the purpose of these books to address all of the moral issues involved; they are simply telling the facts. If you want to read about these events from a moral perspective, then you must read the prophets. The prophets served a couple of very important roles in Israel, as well as in the Bible. They usually came denouncing the immoralities of a nation, calling upon it to repent. They condemned things like offering children as human sacrifices and neglecting widows and orphans. If the call to repentance was ignored, then destruction was threatened. If the threat was ignored, then it was carried out. The biblical view is that God does mean what he says, and the acts of destruction are seen as justice being carried out. It was very much like capital punishment.

We should also notice that violent actions are sometimes presented for the purpose of informing readers of the nature of the times. To present a fact of history is not necessarily the same as endorsing it. Facts are facts whether we like them or not.

Most of us do not object to violence in movies, but to unnecessary violence. We object to violence being glorified. The Bible does address adult themes—incest, rape, murder—but not for the purpose of glorifying these actions.

When our country went to war against Germany and Japan, we did so for moral reasons. Innocent people were dying. One could even make the argument that we waited too long, as it wasn't until we were personally attacked that we joined our European allies. The question is not did we commit an act of violence in entering the war, but rather was there a reason for such involvement? In the same sense, the violence depicted throughout the Old Testament should be examined based upon presentation and purpose rather than upon a natural revulsion for violence in general. So the question is not merely about violence in the Old Testament, but the purpose of that violence and the way it is presented.

I hope all is going well with your pregnancy.

Your friend,
Gene

SOUNDINGS

1. Discuss the difference between violence in a war movie and violence in a slasher movie?

2. Does the Bible condemn all war as immoral? Support your answer.

3. Is it right for a Christian to go to war or work as a police officer? Defend your answer.

CAPITAL PUNISHMENT

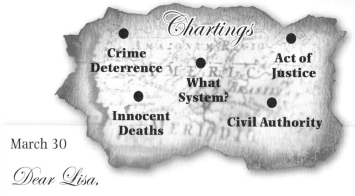

Chartings

- Crime Deterrence
- Act of Justice
- What System?
- Innocent Deaths
- Civil Authority

March 30

Dear Lisa,

I assume you and Blaine have been giving a lot of thought to what you are going to name the baby. I think sitting around thumbing through books full of names for babies is one of the most enjoyable parts of having a child. Just remember this: whatever name you pick, when children get old enough they will tell you what they wish you had named them.

Well, my comments on war have raised another issue in your mind. My comparing much of the Old Testament violence to capital punishment brings to mind your reservations about the death penalty. As I read your remarks it occurred to me that you really don't seem to be opposed to the concept of capital punishment so much as you are concerned with the way it is carried out. Your objections to the practice seem to fall into two categories: (1) you fear innocent people have been put to death, and (2) capital punishment does not deter crime.

I share your concerns about the possibility of innocent people being executed. Undoubtedly some innocent people have been put to death. That thought is one that should bother anyone with a conscience. The possibility of executing an innocent person has led us to a rather cumbersome judicial process in capital cases.

As for your second reason, capital punishment not being a deterrent to crime, the Bible views that as a non-issue. Since, as you have correctly surmised, the Bible does sanction capital punishment, let's run through the teaching of Scripture on the subject.

The book of Leviticus lists more than 20 different capital offenses. In addition to murder, homosexuality, incest, and adultery, other sexual crimes such as bestiality were also punishable by death. As I have already mentioned, Israel was a theocracy, therefore the law of the Old Testament contained both religious and civil regulations. The Old Covenant recognized the possibility that innocent people could be tried for capital crimes, so there were three important safeguards toward that end. First, no one could be condemned to die based on the testimony of one person (Deuteronomy 17:6). The death penalty required two or even three witnesses. Perhaps just as important as the two-or-three-witness requirement was the fact that perjury (called "bearing false witness") was also punishable by death (Deuteronomy 19:15–21). I suspect that had a tendency to reduce the numbers of people willing to frame an innocent party.

One final barrier the law erected to protect innocent parties from being put to death was that judges had some discretion in the matter of sentencing. The very fact that it took "two or three" witnesses seems to indicate two witnesses might not always be enough. Also, there are a number of occasions in which people were guilty of capital crimes, but the death penalty was not administered. Mercy was always an option.

I must admit I have often thought it would make a difference in our judicial system if witnesses, prosecutors, and defense attorneys had to operate today under a system that made them subject to the possibility of dying for their deceptions.

As for whether or not the death penalty is a deterrent to crime, the idea seldom receives attention in the Bible for one simple reason: capital punishment is seen as an act of justice rather than deterrence. In the book of Genesis it is put this way: "Whoever sheds man's blood, by man his blood shall be shed; for in the image of God He made man" (Genesis 9:6). The entire legal system of the Old Testament was built on the premise of justice, not deterrence. The murderer could be sentenced to die because death was deemed a just penalty for the crime. How that penalty might affect the behavior of others was not even given consideration. The famous maxim "an eye for an eye" was simply calling for justice, though many people have misconstrued that statement as giving injured parties the right to exact vengeance. That law made sure no one received a penalty beyond what their crime deserved, so it protected both the criminal and the injured party.

One of the few biblical statements regarding deterrence is in Ecclesiastes 8:11: "Because the sentence against an evil work is not executed speedily, therefore the heart of the sons of men is fully set in them to do evil." From the biblical perspective, a failure to execute justice in a timely fashion causes some to commit crimes justice might have prevented.

The New Testament is not a civil law, so its teaching on the death penalty is a bit different. In Romans 13 the Bible teaches that the purpose of civil government is to reward good citizens and punish those who do evil (vv. 1–4). The statement that the government "does not bear the sword in vain" is an apparent recognition of the fact that governments might inflict capital punishment without moral impropriety. Nowhere does the New Testament set forth a list of crimes and the punishments they deserve. That question is left up to civil authorities.

I hope this sets your mind at ease—as much as one's mind may be at ease about such a matter—concerning what the Bible teaches about capital punishment.

Your friend,
Gene

SOUNDINGS

1. In your opinion should the death penalty be used in our system of justice? Under what circumstances could you sentence someone to death?

2. Discuss the idea that the death penalty should not be used because an innocent person might accidentally be condemned.

3. What do you think about the safeguards in Israel's code of justice to prevent innocent people from receiving the death penalty? Will those safeguards work today? Defend your answer.

9

Additional Moral Issues

CRUELTY TO ANIMALS

Chartings

- **Revolting Sacrifices**
- **Animals' Sabbath**
- **Symbols of Sin**
- **My Crimes**

April 6

Dear Lisa,

How is your mother doing? Is her therapy helping?

Your last letter caught me a bit off-guard. Knowing the number and variety of animals you have, I probably should have been expecting a question about the biblical view of the treatment of animals, but it is not a question I am asked very often. I can see where someone who loves animals as you do would be concerned.

Israel's civil law included regulations about the humane treatment of animals. In Proverbs a righteous man is said to be one who "regards the life of his animal" (Proverbs 12:10). The importance of not working on the Sabbath day is a well-known aspect of the Old Testament law, however, the Sabbath was a day of rest not only for people, but also for their animals (Exodus 23:12). The law obligated people to help animals that had fallen under their burden (Exodus 23:5). The working animal was declared worthy of enjoying the fruits of its labor, therefore an ox threshing grain was not allowed to be muzzled (Deuteronomy 25:4). And Jesus agreed that a donkey or an ox that had fallen into a ditch was to be helped, even on the Sabbath day (Luke 14:5). Clearly the Bible does not condone the mistreatment of animals.

Most specifically, you seemed to be bothered by the idea of animal sacrifices. It is important that we address this matter because I believe it is a crucial part of the biblical teaching about salvation. You find the idea of offering animal sacrifices "revolting." In all fairness it should be mentioned that many of these sacrifices were eaten by the priests, so it was not the wasteful practice you may have imagined.

I am actually glad you find the idea of animal lives being taken disgusting, because that is exactly the point. We are supposed to feel sorrow for the animal because it is giving its innocent life on behalf of a guilty party. God's declaration from the beginning was that the just penalty for sin is forfeiture of the transgressor's life. The reason so much emphasis is placed on the blood of the sacrificed animal is because of the understanding that the "life is in the blood." The sinner has forfeited his life, thus it is life that must be taken to atone for his sins. These animals were not offered because God needed the sacrifice. They were offered to keep vivid before the human race the consequences of their sins. Of course, all of this was a prelude to God's ultimate sacrifice in giving the life of his Son for our sins.

In short, the horror we see and feel at the slaughter of an animal is supposed to be transferred to our own crimes. Sin cannot be ignored. The animal reminds us that someone or something must pay the price for our sins.

Thank you for bringing this issue to my attention.

Your friend,
Gene

Soundings

1. Do animal sacrifices constitute cruelty to animals? Defend your answer.

2. Discuss the Old Testament laws regarding the proper treatment of animals.

3. Discus the modern view of animal rights in light of the biblical view.

ENVIRONMENTALISM

Chartings

Creator vs. Creation

Caretakers

Nature Is God?

Respect

April 12

Dear Lisa,

I do hope your mother gets her wish and lives to see her grandchild. The doctor's prognosis is not good, but unusual things often happen in these situations, especially, I believe, with prayer.

Our conversations have really opened my eyes to the changing landscape Christians must be prepared to walk. When it comes to talking with people about the credibility of Christianity, most of us think in terms of Christianity versus competing religious movements of the world. But you are raising some very different issues, and I suspect these are matters we need to be prepared to answer.

Your questions about Christianity and the environment present the challenge of determining what biblical principles might apply to the subject. The environmental movement and concerns about various forms of pollution are rather unique to industrialized times.

I doubt the green earth movement had much of a following in first-century Jerusalem.

When it comes to how religious movements view nature, there is a lot of variation. Those philosophies that are often pointed to as being "nature friendly" are often pantheistic, meaning their followers believe nature is God. They believe God is the trees, the animals, the oceans, the rivers, and the sky. This invariably leads to worshiping nature. The biblical perspective is very clear: God is the Creator and is to be distinguished from the creation, just as the carpenter should not be confused with a chair or table made with his hands. But differentiating between God and the creation does not mean Christians do not respect the creation.

Another concern you mentioned is a fear that the biblical view of life in another world might lead to a lack of concern for the planet. That is a bit of a leap. I can honestly say I have never met a fellow believer who advocated trashing the environment because he planned to go to heaven. Most have a vested interest in clean water and air as our children and grandchildren will be here long after we are gone. Besides, just because I'll have another car one day doesn't mean I'll abuse the one I have, especially if I am planning on handing my old car down to my daughter.

Please remember that Christians also believe they will receive a wonderful new body in the resurrection. Yet, the doctrine of the resurrection doesn't encourage us to abuse the bodies we have now. To the contrary, Christianity teaches us to be even more respectful of our bodies because they are temples of God called to a higher purpose (1 Corinthians 6:12–20).

From the biblical perspective, this planet has an exalted place—a possession of God on loan to humanity. The Bible never describes the earth as a property which humans are free to abuse; rather, God has made us caretakers of his property. Jesus gave a parable about a man who left his household in the care of his servants. The householder was very displeased with those who did not take care of the things he left in their care (Luke 12:41–48).

Another principle of Christianity addresses environmental concerns, and that is wastefulness. The Bible encourages Christians to make wise use of their resources, whatever they are. We are to use our money and abilities wisely; our abilities are to be utilized properly. When Jesus miraculously fed large crowds, he ordered his disciples to collect the leftovers (Matthew 14:13–21; 15:32–39).

So while it is true that Christianity is not at all in sympathy with those who wish to make a god out of nature, neither does it condone wastefulness or carelessness, whatever the variety may be.

Your friend,
Gene

SOUNDINGS

1. Read Romans 1:18–32. Did the sinful conduct begin when men confused the Creator with the creation? How does one's concept of God relate to one's standard of morality?

2. What does Genesis 3:21 teach about the roles of animals and man?

3. What other biblical principles address environmentalism?

ARE CHRISTIANS HOMOPHOBIC?

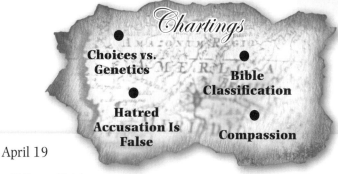

Chartings

- Choices vs. Genetics
- Bible Classification
- Hatred Accusation Is False
- Compassion

April 19

Dear Lisa,

Naming your baby girl after your mother is a thoughtful act. Though she protested when you presented the idea, I'm sure somewhere there was a glow of delight. It is, after all, one of the greatest tributes you can pay a person.

Obviously, you and Blaine changed your mind and opted to learn the sex of the baby. Isn't it funny how quickly we can change our minds about such things?

Your most recent question leads us into several different areas, and I'm not sure where to start. The teachings of the Bible on the subject of homosexuality have been the source of a lot of "bad press." Accusations of "hate-mongering" and "homophobia" made against religious groups that teach the practice is incompatible with Christian conduct are very serious charges. But your questions are bold and to the point, so I shall make every effort to be just as forthright in my responses.

Lisa, I cannot address the claims your lesbian co-worker makes about mistreatment by Christians. I cannot address them because I have no personal knowledge of them. And as you well know, the difference between actually being abused and being overly sensitive is often difficult to judge. However, I will be happy to deal with the information she has given you insofar as I am able, as well as presenting the biblical teaching on the matter.

To get right to the point, Christians believe homosexual conduct is sinful because the Bible classifies it as such. In Romans 1:24–28 homosexual practices are said to be "against nature," "shameful," and the product of "a debased mind." There have been several efforts over the past few years to reinterpret biblical statements condemning homosexual behavior so that the two might appear compatible, but the Bible is so plain-spoken on the subject, until recently very few have taken these new interpretations seriously. The Bible really is consistent on the matter. Whether you look into the Old Testament or the New, homosexuality is clearly considered an unacceptable practice.

Of all of the charges, claims, and accusations being made against the Christian community, there is one that stands above all of the rest: Christian opposition to homosexuality is a form of hatred. If I seem a bit passionate or emotional at this point, please understand that it has nothing to do with any extra-ordinary disdain for homosexuals, but because the Christian community has been falsely charged.

The problem is quite simple: the Christian's non-acceptance of the practices of homosexuals has been portrayed as hatred for the practitioners. I cannot help but believe such a portrayal has more to do with politics than it does with hatred on the part of most Christian people.

What is hatred? As I understand it, hatred is the desire for harm to come to another individual. The Christian people with whom I am familiar do not feel that way toward those who practice homosexuality.

This concept is not difficult to understand. All of us daily face conduct of which we do not approve, but personal hatred for the individuals involved is not a necessary element of the disapproval. You may dislike the conduct of a man who recklessly exceeds the speed limit, but does that mean you hate him? You may express your disapproval for people who rob houses for a living without meaning you hate all robbers.

In the Bible, homosexuality is one of several sexual activities deemed sinful. Bestiality, incest, pedophilia, adultery, and heterosexual relations outside marriage are all immoral acts from which Christians must abstain. To many it appears that homosexual sins receive a bit more resistance than heterosexual ones. Perhaps so, but no coalition of heterosexual fornicators has been demanding churches accept their conduct or be maligned as hateful. I can assure you that if a group calling itself People United for Fornication

(PUFF) began referring to churches that refuse to accept their activities as full of hatred, you would see the same kind of resistance.

There seems to have been an attempt to create a no-win situation for the Christian community. Christians are told they must either endorse homosexual conduct or be considered hateful. Neither is a very nice alternative.

A lot of attention is being given to the source of homosexual behavior. Your colleague has told you many times she did not choose to be homosexual; rather, she was born that way. Does this mean the biblical view that homosexual conduct is immoral is simply a relic of past ignorance? Many who believe that homosexuality is biologically determined have taken this view of the Bible.

The most common reason for believing homosexuality is not a choice is that no one would willingly choose a conduct that leads to the abuse the homosexual community claims. But this is simply not true. Early Christians had their homes confiscated, faced imprisonment, and often faced death simply because they were Christians. No one would dare advance the idea that they were Christians for any reason other than personal choice. I do not believe there is any individual viewed with deeper disdain in our society than a rapist, but the fact that evil men continually commit that crime does not mean they were born rapists. It is a choice. Does this mean I want homosexuals thrown into jail? Not at all; I am simply showing that this particular line of reasoning does not prove homosexuality is anything but a choice.

I noticed that your friend also cited a number of scientific studies that she believes prove homosexuality is biologically determined. I cannot even begin to address all of the studies. Besides, many of them have already been proved false.

But none of this addresses the real point. Let us suppose sexual orientation is determined by a combination of environmental and genetic factors. It is also claimed, for example, that some people have a genetic predisposition to alcohol addiction. That doesn't mean they are born alcoholics. And even if it is true that a person's alcoholism has genetic connections, that doesn't change the fact that he needs to be helped out of his self-destructive behavior. Considering the significantly shortened lifespan of individuals in the homosexual community, along with the high rate of sexually transmitted diseases and suicide, is it really all that difficult to believe homosexuality is an abnormal, self-destructive life-style?

Compassion is sometimes tough. The person who truly has compassion on the alcoholic does not condone his behavior but holds out hope for a better way of life. When we look at it in this light, perhaps the truly compassionate people are those who hold out the hope that the homosexual can change, rather than making him the helpless victim of biology.

My prayers continue to be with you as you look after your mother and prepare to enter the joys of parenting.

Your friend,
Gene

SOUNDINGS

1. If there is a genetic component to homosexuality, does that prove the Bible is wrong in marking homosexuality as sinful? Discuss your answer in view of the Bible's position on drunkenness, even for the alcoholic.

2. Are those who call for alcoholics to abstain from drinking lacking compassion? Are they being mean or hateful? Defend your answers.

3. Some argue that since homosexual conduct is sometimes persecuted, and since no one would willingly choose to be persecuted, then homosexual conduct is not a choice. Discuss the validity of this argument.

CHRISTIANS AND ABORTION

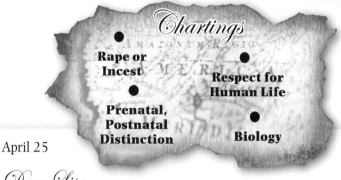

Chartings

- Rape or Incest
- Respect for Human Life
- Prenatal, Postnatal Distinction
- Biology

April 25

Dear Lisa,

Your interesting comments about abortion show how much our circumstances can alter our views. Your previous position was firmly supportive of abortion on demand, but that all changed during a recent birthing class as you witnessed the stomach of one of the mothers moving. You realized your little Sandra will soon be doing the same gymnastics inside you. Disturbing doubts began to intrude on your convictions.

I, too, was once firmly in favor of abortion for any reason, so I am aware of the turmoil you feel. My change of conviction on the matter was for both biblical and non-biblical reasons. I will be happy to share with you my understanding of the abortion issue, and I hope it helps you find peace of mind.

From a biblical perspective there is no explicit prohibition against abortion. Of course, if one comes to the conviction that the unborn constitute human life, then biblical statements against taking innocent human life would apply. But even the question of whether or not the yet-to-be-born are human is a bit tricky, since there is no direct biblical statement regarding the matter.

So how is one supposed to reach the proper conclusion? For me it isn't that the Bible makes a big issue out of the status of the unborn so much as the fact that it makes no distinction at all between prenatal and postnatal children. The born and the not-yet-born are spoken of in the same way. John the Baptist was simply called a babe when he leaped in his mother's womb (Luke 1:41). Jesus was called a babe as he lay in a manger (Luke 2:12). The lack of recognizing any difference between the born and the unborn implies that there is no difference between the two.

But I must be honest and admit that my "conversion" did not begin with biblical considerations at all. After much contemplation I came to the inescapable conclusion that the unborn constitutes human life by its very nature. Two human beings have never produced anything but another human (Genesis 1:28). The facts of biology led me to wonder why anyone including myself would assume the unborn were ever anything but human. Granted, the appearance of the unborn changes at various stages of development, but not being fully developed did not seem to be reason enough to deny they are human. If all things reproduce after their kind, then it logically follows that the result of two human beings is another human being, regardless of the stage of development. The most uncomfortable position is one that tries to decide at which stage of growth the living mass becomes human. The truth is, we continue to develop for years after we are born.

Lisa, abortion has always been a very divisive and emotional subject, but the debate has changed in a nasty way over the past several years. I can remember hearing countless discussions over whether or not the unborn were human. But the common practice of partial-birth abortion has made it clear that many people have no objection to destroying human life, for no one can deny the humanness of a partially delivered baby. So, I fear, what we are left with is a greatly diminished respect for human life. That makes me sad.

You asked me if I believe it is ever right to have an abortion. In cases where the mother's life is in danger, then a choice as to who lives obviously must be made. But as long as both are capable of surviving the birth process, I see no reason for terminating one any more than the other. It is an issue of human life; I cannot consistently believe differently.

The scary question is one you brought up about pregnancies resulting from rape or incest. Since I have come to believe the unborn are human, it would seem grossly inconsistent for me to say it would be all right to abort in those situations. At the same time, I freely admit I would hate to be in the position of explaining to a victim why she ought to deliver the baby. The only consolation on this question is that the trauma involved in rape and incest makes conception a very rare thing. If the only abortions were performed as a result of rape and incest, the number would be very small indeed.

I hope my phone call the other day didn't seem unduly pushy. I do so enjoy our correspondence, and when I didn't hear from you in what has come to be the usual lapse of time I became concerned there was a problem with your mother or the baby. I know it must have sent waves of panic through you when you had to take your mom to the hospital again. Please take your doctor's advice and stay off your feet as much as possible so that you may avoid premature delivery.

Your friend,
Gene

SOUNDINGS

1. Has abortion ever been discussed in your school experience? What conclusions were drawn?

2. Regarding unwanted pregnancies, what options are available other than abortion? Discuss some of the difficulties the birth of a baby brings to a woman's life.

3. Discuss the pros and cons of abortions in cases of rape and incest.

10

Christianity and Science

EVOLUTION AND THE AGE OF THE EARTH

Chartings

● Theory vs. Fact

● Faith Either Way

● Extent of Evolvement

● Speculation

May 1

Dear Lisa,

Thank you for your recent letter. I was fascinated with the newspaper article regarding the ancient remains found in Central Africa. The study of early man has interested me for quite some time.

You underlined a sentence you found of particular interest, and you wonder if the Bible can be reconciled to the scientific facts contained in the sentence. Since you sent me the article I will assume you no longer have a copy, so I will reproduce the sentence for you to jog your memory. The sentence said: "The remains are believed to be about 100,000 years old and may be an example of an early ancestor of man." Your first question was: "Can the Bible be reconciled to the earth being several billion years old?" Your second question was: "Can the Bible be reconciled with the evolution of life?"

You have attributed more to this find than did the author of the article. You referred to the information contained in the sentence as "scientific facts." However, the article says, "The remains are *believed* to be *about* 100,000 years old and *may* be an example of an early ancestor of man." The statements made about the find are very cautiously worded, which is understandable since the find is quite recent. Much more study must be done before releasing any definite conclusions. Premature claims of similar finds have proved embarrassing when the claims were later found to be false.

It is important that we carefully distinguish between fact and theory. I think most scientists would agree with me on that point. The only true fact we have in the article was that skeletal remains were found in Central Africa. The bones themselves are facts. Where they were found is a fact. But since terms like "believed," "about," and "may" were used to describe the rest of the information given, they do not qualify as facts, at least not yet.

Another matter about which we as readers must be careful is drawing too many conclusions from an article written for popular consumption. Newspaper reports of scientific investigations usually include speculative conclusions, but they provide the reader with meager evidence. If the conclusion is based on statistics we seldom see the raw data, just what people have made of the data. To get conclusive information requires a lot more digging, something most people are unwilling to do. For example, the article you sent me says only that human-like skeletal remains were found in Central Africa. But of what did these remains consist? Most people probably envision something like the skeleton hanging in their college physiology classroom with all of the bones neatly intact, but that is seldom the case. An entire skeleton is rarely found and, quite often, only very few bones are found. Some finds consist of a few teeth and part of the jawbone. Obviously, the conclusions are greatly affected by the size and condition of the sample.

Both theology and science have suffered great embarrassment because they got dogmatic when they should have been cautious. Theologians have been reminded about the Roman Catholic Church forcing Galileo's recantation of his then-novel theory that the sun and not the earth is the center of our solar system. That is a silly game neither side should want to play, as many alleged proofs of the evolution of man have later been shown false. One example is that of the "Nebraska Man." His teeth were later identified as a pig's teeth! In the end, this kind of thing doesn't seem to aid our search for truth.

Can the Bible be reconciled to the *facts* of science? I believe it can. The Bible and the *interpretations* and *theories* science places on the facts often do not agree, but the facts themselves do not present a problem.

Specifically you asked about the Bible and the theory of evolution. I do not think there is any doubt that living things have evolved. Even in our own life time we have seen new variations brought about through selective breeding. The real question is not have living things evolved, but to what *extent* have they evolved? The biblical account is pretty generic in this area. We are told land animals, birds, fish, plants, and insects were created, but the extent to which the variations within these categories were created is left unanswered (Genesis 1–2). So the idea that living things have evolved is not necessarily in conflict with the Bible, though certain specific ideas maintained by certain scientists may not square very well. When you get past generalities and start dealing with the specifics of the theory of evolution, you find a wide divergence of opinion among evolutionists.

As for the age of the earth, that is an interesting question. Science has used many different methods to try to determine the age for our planet. Just about any rate of change that may be considered somewhat uniform has been applied to this question. Both the rate of decay of the earth's magnetic field and the formation of rivers' deltas have been used. A great variety of results have been gleaned from hundreds of different methods. So how old is the earth? The Bible doesn't attempt to answer that question, and I don't believe modern science can answer it, either.

So I do not believe one must make a choice between believing in the facts of science or the Bible since they are not in conflict with one another.

Your friend,
Gene

SOUNDINGS

1. What is a fact? Should the theory of evolution be taught as a fact in our public schools? Defend your answer.

2. How should the origin of life be presented without bias in public schools?

3. What should both science and religion learn from their past mistakes regarding the origin of life and the creation of the universe?

EVOLUTION IS UNNATURAL

Chartings

Biologically Moral?

Natural vs. Supernatural

Animals without Conscience

Chaos to Order?

May 7

Dear Lisa,

Let me be clear about this: I do not claim to be a biological scientist. In fact, I am at a distinct disadvantage as I discuss theories of origins with you, a science teacher. At the same time, I am able to observe the world around me, and what I see does not seem to fit with the idea that all life is the result of a single lower life-form that has been gradually improving through the ages due to a series of accidents.

Evolution is set forth as a natural explanation for life without having to resort to the supernatural. Now I suppose for the many reared on the idea that biological life has been improving incrementally for eons such sounds natural, even normal. But Lisa, stop and think about this for a moment: Can you come up with even one example where chaos turned into order all by itself? I have racked my brain on this one and, frankly, not even one example has come to my mind. The effects of accidents on chaos always seem to be something more chaotic. Yet, it is my understanding that the very foundation of evolutionary theory is that a series of accidents (called mutations) in the midst of a chaotic mess not only produced the first life, but subsequently improved it to the levels we see about us. It all seems very unnatural to me.

I never see life coming from anything but previous life, which is exactly what the Bible says we should expect (Genesis 1:20–25). I once read of a very learned fellow who asserted that evolution can be seen in the way a seed can produce a large plant that is nothing like the seed. But the seed came from a previous plant. What I would need to observe to convince me otherwise is something non-living producing something with life. That ought to be the natural order if evolution is the natural explanation for life.

There is another matter that just doesn't seem to fit the idea of life owing its existence to a series of mindless biological accidents: How did such a mindless process produce moral thinking?

Lisa, I know you have a very strong set of moral values. You have mentioned to me how people ought to be kinder to each other. Why? There are some very mean people in the world. What is your basis for telling them to be nice? Is it purely because your neurological impulses say so? And since they have the same kind of impulses telling them to be mean, what makes your impulses morally superior to theirs? Does our sense of moral right and wrong run no deeper than biological processes?

Suppose for a moment that the judges in our courts suddenly started siding with the mean people. What could you say to them if morality is merely the result of biochemical processes?

As I observe my fellow human beings, I see creatures with some definite ideas about how people ought to behave so as not to harm others. I see people inconveniencing themselves to help the weaker. I see people refusing to do what they want to do in order to do what they ought to do. I conclude that such impulses are not natural, therefore they are supernatural in origin. The difference seems to be what we call a conscience. For some reason we humans seem to be the only animals on the planet with a built-in mechanism that condemns us when we violate the moral law. I wonder why no other animals evolved a conscience? I cannot explain the human conscience without resorting to a supernatural explanation.

In short, if our moral values are simply the result of biochemical processes, then they have the same origin as a bad case of indigestion. That seems very unnatural.

Your friend,
Gene

SOUNDINGS

1. Give one example, if you can, of chaos turned into order all by itself without any outside interference.

2. Give an example, if you can, of non-life producing a living organism.

3. When someone kills another human being, is that act wrong only because we have evolved the idea that killing is wrong? If we evolved the idea that it is all right to kill another human being, would it then be all right? Discuss your conclusions.

11

Christianity and Gender Roles

DIVORCE

Chartings

- No-Fault?
- Moral or Practical?
- Personal Happiness?
- Narrow?

May 13

Dear Lisa,

It was good to hear things have stabilized and the doctors are confident you will be able to carry Sandra to full term. I know it is quite stressful to watch your mother's health deteriorate. I know you have a desire to do everything you can to make her life a little easier. I hope it will not seem as though I am interfering, but you need to allow your mother to see to her own needs as long as she is able. She will soon have to swallow her pride and ask for help. You will have much opportunity to care for her then.

I'm sure it must be confusing when Christians give you conflicting ideas of what Christianity teaches in certain areas. Your instincts, however, are right: the Bible most definitely discourages divorce. In fact, in one place it is even written that God hates divorce (Malachi 2:16). The general teaching of Scripture is that a man and woman marry for life. The exception given to that general rule is when one's mate is guilty of adultery (Matthew 19:3–12).

As to whether or not this idea seems rather narrow or may infringe on one's pursuit of happiness, those are indeed interesting topics of discussion.

I must frankly admit that the charge of a belief or philosophy being too narrow doesn't impress me very much. To dismiss something because it seems to leave little latitude for personal action doesn't address the bigger questions of whether or not the idea is morally right or even practically superior. To call an idea narrow or to refer to someone as narrow-minded usually means nothing more than, "I disagree with your rejection of my beliefs or practices."

Attitudes toward divorce have changed a lot over the years. I know you realize this from the way you spoke of the 40-year marriage of your own parents. Your parents had difficult periods that easily could have led to divorce, but they had made a commitment to each other and their children, so they stayed married and dealt with their differences. It was only the untimely accidental death of your father that separated them.

When I was a boy I remember hearing people talk about whether or not someone had grounds for divorce and how they might go about proving their case. Since the advent of no-fault divorce, such discussions are no longer necessary. Now all one needs to get a divorce is apply for one. So it is true the biblical teachings on marriage and divorce are much more narrow than the practices of modern society, but I think you will have a difficult time proving this broader view has really added to the happiness of most divorcees. Getting one's own way and being happy about it are two very different concepts. Getting what one wants is often the first step toward misery.

Lisa, do you honestly believe the increase in the divorce rate has resulted in greater happiness for our society? I think we both realize that most children growing up without both a mom and a dad at home are at a disadvantage. Your own experience as a school teacher has surely taught you that.

The biblical view of marriage is not merely about a husband and wife; rather, it takes into account the whole family. According to the Bible, rearing children is a job best accomplished by two people. Two people are required to create children, and that is not an accident of nature. However, God forbids procreative activities except in marriage. That this arrangement works best is apparent when one compares the academic and economic statistics of children reared in two-parent homes with those brought up in one-parent homes.

Does all of this mean the child from a single-parent home is without hope? Of course not. Single parenthood is not always by choice, as is the case in the death of a parent. Sometimes a parent's conduct is such that he or she should be removed from the family—habitual marital unfaithfulness, domestic violence, alcohol and drug abuse, and other degrading behaviors. But these situations hardly establish the general premise that divorce is beneficial for families or society.

We all want personal happiness, so we build roads we think will lead us to that goal. But roads need maintaining, and that is the part most people don't like. People tend to want a shortcut to happiness. Most people believe that peace and happiness should require no effort on their part, and any idea that involves work cannot possibly lead to happiness. So people get married because they believe it will provide a road to happiness. When the road gets a few bumps or ruts, rather than resurface it they decide to build a new road. Unfortunately, those who spend their lives building new roads never finish any one of them, so they never reach their destination of happiness. That is sad but true.

I hope things continue to go well with your pregnancy.

Your friend,
Gene

SOUNDINGS

1. Contrast the merits of specific-grounds divorce and no-fault divorce.

2. Should personal happiness be our main goal in life? If not, what should our goal in life be?

3. What kind of work is required to obtain peace and happiness?

MEN AND WOMEN HAVE GOD-GIVEN ROLES

Chartings

- Definite Roles
- Newspaper Sources
- Reflections of Reality
- Instincts

May 20

Dear Lisa,

I am so glad you received a favorable report from your obstetrician. It sounds like Sandra is coming along quite nicely. I'm sure the doctor's advice to stay off your feet is difficult to follow, but be patient: Sandra will be out of the oven before you know it.

Is the nursery ready yet? The shower next week will provide gifts that you need.

I, too, read the newspaper article about a religious group recently affirming male leadership. Remember our discussion of the fossil find in Africa. A newspaper article is not a good place to get your science; neither is it a good source for theology.

I must decline your invitation to comment on the article. It is so vague that I cannot make any meaningful statements without making many assumptions about what this group was affirming. Most articles of this nature provide only enough information to inflame the passions of some who don't really understand the beliefs of the group in question.

Rather than comment on the article, I would prefer to set forth my understanding of what the Bible teaches about gender roles. Let's look at this subject from two perspectives, first noting what the Bible teaches about male leadership and the roles of men and women in the home, then looking at how this plays out in everyday life.

The New Testament teaches that the basic role of the woman in the family is that of nurturer and care giver (Titus 2:3–5), while the man's basic role is that of provider and protector (Ephesians

5:25–29). I know this sounds a little old fashioned to many, but it is a model that has served the human race well for many centuries. It also appeals to reason when one understands that from the biblical perspective men and women are different both physically and emotionally. While our physical differences are too obvious to deny, many do deny that men and women are inherently different emotionally. They believe any differences are purely environmental. We raise boys to have masculine qualities and girls to have feminine ones.

I don't need to convince you. You have demonstrated by written and spoken words that your belief on this matter is the same as mine. You recently spoke of your own "nesting instinct" when you and Blaine decided to conceive a child. You described your desire to have a baby as a "need," whereas for Blaine it was more like a "want." Women are more nurturing than men are—a gift from the Creator. Therefore, the Bible describes the role of the woman as primarily domestic and that of the man as working outside the home (Genesis 3:16–19). If you accept the view that the way children are conceived, born, and reared is by design and not merely an accident of nature, then it is easy to see how this process reflects the biblical portrayal of men and women in the family.

I remember when my father and I stayed with one of our mares late into the night, waiting to help her deliver. We gave up and went to bed. The next morning the new filly was walking around and finding her way to her mother's milk. Within six months it no longer needed its mother at all. Even animals with life spans closer to that of humans develop much faster. Elephants live about seventy years, but after a mere four years the calf is its own.

Humans, the most intelligent of all animals, require the most nurturing. A horse is self-sufficient in half the time it takes a human baby to learn to walk. And while an elephant requires a longer period of nurturing than a horse, a four-year-old child wouldn't stand much of a chance of making it on its own. Someone must spend much time nurturing a human child. Again, if we assume things are by design rather than accident, the woman is the logical one to fulfill the domestic role since she is equipped both physically and emotionally to provide that care. Since the woman's talents are required in the domestic realm, the primary role of the man is, of necessity, outside the domestic arena as provider. In other words, the biblical teaching of the roles of men and women in family life are simply a reflection of the reality of the situation.

Since the Bible recognizes different roles in the home, does that mean it is wrong for a woman to have a job outside the home? Of course not. The Bible does not forbid a woman's working outside the home any more than it forbids a man's doing the dishes. But the man and the woman must never lose sight of their primary focuses.

When I started this letter, I intended to address more issues. But I now think I should stop and provide you an opportunity to raise questions or request clarification on some of the above matters.

Don't forget to rest and take your vitamins.

Your friend,
Gene

SOUNDINGS

1. Discuss the advantages for children of two-parent households. What can we do to help families with only one parent in the home?

2. Are the emotional differences of men and women inherent or are they the result of having been treated differently as children? Defend your answer.

3. Do most women really have a "nesting instinct"? Defend your answer.

GENDER EQUALITY

Chartings

No Equality
in Abilities

Bible Limitations

Superiority
vs. Authority

Leadership

May 28

Dear Lisa,

It sounds as if you had a great time at the baby shower as well as getting some very useful things. You may find our gift of the baby monitor redundant since new mothers seem to be walking, breathing baby monitors. As a newlywed, my wife could sleep through anything. But after our first child was born, the slightest sound from the nursery would wake her and prompt a quick peek into the crib. Many other women have related similar experiences to me. I guess it is just another one of those built-in mothering instincts.

I am so glad that your mother felt well enough to attend the shower and share that moment with you. I should imagine that in her condition she has very few ordinary moments, but I'm sure the shower was a special time for both of you.

I think you are right; the thoughts presented in my last letter are things upon which most women agree, especially those who have experienced motherhood. I suspect that motherhood has given a new attitude even to a few of the more radical feminists.

The issue that you believe most women find objectionable is that of male leadership or headship. You believe that a marriage works best when it is a 50-50 proposition. Furthermore, since it is the male leadership notion that bars women from various duties in some churches, you maintain it is bound to be a major point of protest among women who refuse to accept Christianity.

Let me give it to you straight: The Bible does teach "the husband is the head of the wife" (Ephesians 5:23). That's about as plain as it could be stated. As for whether or not some roles in the church are retained exclusively for men, the Bible says that in order to be a bishop one must be "the husband of one wife" (1 Timothy 3:2). That pretty well limits that position to men only.

Our society has changed a lot with regard to gender roles, and it gets more difficult to speak with people about this issue and feel as though they have really listened. Probably the greatest example of this is the major effort to place women in military combat situations traditionally handled exclusively by men. All of this is done in the name of equality. Frankly, I believe the call for equality has gone mad when it fails to recognize the physical and emotional differences between men and women. Just as women are specially equipped, both physically and emotionally, to fulfill the domestic role, men, by virtue of their superior physical strength and tendency toward a more violent nature, are better suited to fulfill the role of protector.

Any talk of equality must leave room for recognizing that one person may be better at one thing than another person is. We all have different talents and we ought to rejoice in the abilities we have rather than demand equal recognition with others in areas where we lack special talents. A good example of this is in a family with two children. Those children are bound to have their own individual strengths and weaknesses: one may be athletic while the other may do superbly well in academic areas. It is rather silly to tell the athlete he is just as good in the classroom as his or her sibling, and there is no sense in telling the scholar he is just as athletic as the other. Wise parents recognize the differing strengths of their children, while seeing them as equal in so far as their human value is concerned. In other words, men and women, like all individuals, are equal in their value, but that does not mean they are equal with respect to abilities, gifts, and talents. Each one has individual strengths and weaknesses.

Because of preconceived ideas, I think many people are prejudiced against male authority. When people on one side of the issue say the word *authority*, the other side seems to hear the word *superiority*. Now under normal conditions we are able to see that authority and human worth are not connected concepts. The policeman who gives you a ticket for breaking a traffic law has authority over you, but you and the officer are equal as human beings. Our politicians pass laws we do not like, thereby exercising their authority over us, but they are not superior human beings before God. I doubt it has ever even crossed our minds to think their authority made them superior members of the human race. Why, then, should we be left to conclude that the Christian doctrine of male leadership means one gender is inferior to the other?

Is it possible for the concept of male leadership to go to a man's head, thus causing him to abuse this God-given distinction? When that happens the man has forgotten the important concept that everybody is under the authority of another. No man has been granted supreme authority, for "the head of every man is Christ" (1 Corinthians 11:3), so when a man does not fulfill his responsibility as the head of his family, he must answer to his head: God! The man who is unwilling to submit to God will probably be a miserable mate.

Your friend,
Gene

SOUNDINGS

1. Must equality between the sexes mean denying there are differences between them?

2. Is it true that men have tendencies toward violence and women toward gentleness? How might each of those qualities serve as a God-given role in the family?

3. Does being under the authority of another mean being inferior to the one in authority? Explain.

Is Christian Marriage Female Bondage?

Chartings

Fully Assembled

Oppressed?

Participant vs. Bystander

Longevity

June 4

Dear Lisa,

Though you have not had an opportunity to respond to my last letter, I wanted to finish my thoughts on gender roles. Sometimes an item looks very different when it sits before us fully assembled rather than as separate pieces in the box. Please consider this letter the completion of my understanding of what the Bible teaches regarding gender roles.

I have a friend who loves to play golf. One day I began to tease him about how unfulfilled an individual's life must be if he finds golf an interesting diversion. His reply was interesting. He said he also used to wonder what could be so entertaining about chasing a little white ball. Then one day he played a round of golf with some friends, and he learned the game appears much different after one changes from spectator to player.

When some women read about male leadership, they cannot imagine marriage being an enjoyable experience. But Christian teachings on marriage and gender roles are a lot like golf: it plays better than it reads and is much different as a participant from what it is as a bystander.

Talk to a married Christian woman and get her perspective on the issue. Ask her if she feels oppressed or under tyrannical rule. Begin with your own mother. You have mentioned several times how wonderful your parents' 40-year marriage was as you witnessed their mutual devotion. Since both of your parents were Christians, I should think their marriage would stand as a pretty good example of the beauty of the biblical teachings on the subject. Did your mom seem oppressed? Did your father seem to be a tyrannical monster?

Here is one final thought. If the biblical concept of marriage and gender roles is so horrifying, why do marriages between Christians have a longevity rate significantly higher than that of the general population?

Your friend,
Gene

SOUNDINGS

1. How should a woman's being under her husband's authority influence her choice of a mate?

2. Have you ever had a discussion with your parents about their marriage? What were their insights?

3. Do most Christian women feel inferior to their husbands? Support your answer.

HUSBANDS ARE LEADERS WHO SERVE

Chartings

Authority
vs. Abuse

Leaders as
Servants

Win-Win
Marriage

Idealistic
Equality

June 12

Dear Lisa,

It truly is an interesting turn of events. Your mother has not only lived a couple of months beyond the doctor's expectations, but she has been taking care of you as of late. Do I attribute this to prayer? I have no way of answering that question without a direct revelation from God himself. I do believe God answers prayer, but it is sometimes difficult for us to know the answer he is giving. My prayers on your mother's behalf have not been so much for a specific outcome; rather, I pray that whatever is in her best interest would come to pass.

I'll bet the discussion you and your mother had about her marriage to your father was a tremendous walk down memory lane. Still, though your parents' marriage had none of the oppression you feared biblical teachings might encourage, you wonder if that is simply because your father did not exercise the kind of authority the Bible gives to men.

Your father very likely exercised the kind of authority the Bible authorizes men to use. Your concept of authority, when it comes to the Bible, seems to assume all people with power are cruel and wish to abuse their power in order to obtain their personal goals. Do you always assume this of someone in authority? Do you believe all police officers wield their authority in this fashion? Frankly, Lisa, as a teacher you have authority, but I would assume you don't see yourself abusing that power. Though some men may use their God-given authority to further a personal agenda, such behavior cannot be biblically justified.

When I began trying to understand your take on Christian male leadership, I had the feeling that you perceived it as that of a drill instructor: someone barking orders. The more I have thought about it, however, your description of Christian male leadership makes a drill instructor look like Mary Poppins, since even a drill instructor, despite his harsh manner, usually has a good reason for his demands. Christian men, per your view, are allowed to yell orders simply because they want things their way.

Here is the key concept you are missing: The Bible depicts leaders as servants. In fact, those with the greatest authority, according to the New Testament, are the greatest servants. Jesus made this point very clear in a memorable way when he washed his disciples' feet: "If I then, your Lord and Teacher, have washed your feet, you also ought to wash one another's feet" (John 13:14). Biblically, Christian leaders do not exercise their authority to elevate themselves, but to be a blessing to others.

We have probably heard of police officers who let their badge, gun, siren, and lights go to their head. But according to the Bible, authority is not a privilege to be exercised so much as a responsibility to be carried. A Christian husband should not ask how his authority can be self-serving, but rather, how does it enable him to serve others better.

You seem to have in mind the possibility of a beautiful world in which no authority exists—everyone is on an equal plane. That might sound nice in theory, but isn't it a bit idealistic? Could an army survive if everyone held the same rank? What would your classroom be like if your students had equal authority with you? Just as roles actually improve the military and the classroom, they also improve the home.

The idea that marriage should be a 50-50 proposition is one I have heard many times. Advocates of that idea haven't spent much time counseling troubled marriages. It has been my experience that partners who see their marriage as a 50-50 situation usually end up as scorekeepers. Both partners begin thinking about how much they have done and now it is about time the other partner did his or her share. This mentality seldom produces marital bliss.

The biblical concept is that marriage is a 100-100 situation. Each is more concerned about the other partner than about himself or herself. I know this doesn't make for good math, but I have found it is far superior to the 50-50 idea. In fact, many marriages described as 50-50 are probably more like the one I am describing. I suspect your parents put the needs of the other above their own.

Christian marriage may well be described as mutual submission. In fact, one of the most controversial passages in the Bible on male leadership begins with the statement: "Submitting to one another in the fear of God" (Ephesians 5:21). How can someone have authority and at the same time be in submission? It's really not all that difficult when the one in authority wants to do what is in the best interest of others.

I realize this may sound a bit confusing, but Christianity never has made much sense when people try to make it fit with non-Christian concepts and definitions.

Your friend,
Gene

SOUNDINGS

1. Discuss the thought that when marriage is seen as a 50-50 proposition people end up being scorekeepers.

2. How does the life of Jesus illustrate a person in authority who is also in submission?

3. What would the world be like if there were no positions of authority?

THE PURPOSE OF SEX

Chartings

- Reasons to be Single
- Affection Due
- Gift to the Married
- Self-Control

June 22

Dear Lisa,

I can't speak from experience, but I am sure this is a miserable time of the year to be pregnant. The heat is incredible.

It has been a long time since anyone asked me whether the Bible teaches that sex is only for procreation. A few religious groups associated with Christianity teach that it is. Most of them, of course, oppose birth control. Neither idea is biblically based; both are merely traditions of those religious movements.

The subject of marriage is addressed in 1 Corinthians 7. That text gives two reasons one might choose not to marry: (1) an unmarried person is able to devote more of his time and energy to religious service (vv. 31–35), and (2) "the present distress" (v. 26). Apparently the persecution of that era was especially hard on Christian families.

Though the Bible says the unmarried have the ability to devote more time to religious service than those who are married, it also notes that an unmarried person is expected to remain celibate, since Christianity teaches that sexual relationships are proper only in the context of marriage. Jesus also noted that the celibate life is not for everyone: "All cannot accept this saying . . . but he who is able to accept it let him accept it" (Matthew 19:11–12).

First Corinthians 7 also teaches that celibacy is not for everyone when it says the person burning with passion should marry. This is not a suggestion that when a person begins to burn lustfully toward someone, he should marry that particular person, but it is a sign that he is "the marrying kind" and does not have the necessary self-control for the celibate life.

Finally, married couples are told not to withhold the sexual relationship from one another for an extended period, and then only by mutual consent lest one be tempted to seek fulfillment elsewhere. The sexual relationship referred to in this context is spoken of as "the affection due" one's mate. Clearly the discussion is about affection and sexual satisfaction and not procreation. The Bible clearly recognizes and advocates sex for recreational purposes.

Since the Bible sanctions recreational sex between a husband and wife, it stands to reason that birth control is acceptable. It should be noted, however, that what some call birth control today is really abortion. The "morning-after" pill may actually kill a life conceived the night before. Couples should investigate the manner in which a contraceptive works before deciding to use it.

The Bible writers, Lisa, were very much aware of the power of the sex drive. They also understood sex was a legitimate form of affection and pleasure, and not merely a way to make babies. Sex is a wonderful gift to the married from God. Sex under other circumstances abuses that gift.

I hope you continue to get good reports at your checkups.

Your friend,
Gene

SOUNDINGS

1. How would not being married give a person more time for things of God?

2. Should one get married just because one is burning in lust? What other options might be available?

3. Must a married couple have as many children as possible? What biblical principles might such an idea violate?

12

Theological Questions

WHY JESUS DIED ON THE CROSS

Chartings

Sowing and Reaping

Forgiveness for All

Only One Qualified

Sin Defined

July 1

Dear Lisa,

It was great seeing you at our worship assembly last Sunday. I hope you found the people friendly. Your mom looked just as proud as she could be to have her daughter with her.

I'm glad you feel comfortable asking questions about the things you heard, especially any confusing ideas in my sermon.

The blood of Christ is something the Bible mentions often, which is why you hear Christians speak about it so much. I hope I can bring some order to the confusion you mentioned over all of the blood sacrifices throughout the Bible.

The Bible teaches that God has always revealed his will to the human race. But then it also teaches that all humans eventually violate the will of God, which is called sin. The word *sin* was a term used to refer to an archer who had missed his target. Thus, when people sin they fail to hit the mark, the mark being God's will.

The Bible is very firm in its teaching that actions have consequences. A famous biblical statement is, "Whatever a man sows, that he will also reap" (Galatians 6:7–8) The consequence of sin is spiritual death, which means one's relationship with God has been changed in such a way that he is no longer in favor with God. One analogy the Bible often uses to describe a person's relationship with God is to say he is either God's friend or his enemy. When we sin we cease to be on a friendship basis with God. Generally speaking, when two people cease to be friends it is because one has wronged the other, and friendship is not restored until forgiveness takes place. The same is true when one sins against God. A sinner needs to be forgiven for his debt of sin. But this forgiveness must be more than merely nodding the head and saying, "Don't worry about it; I forgive you." This will never do because real crimes have been committed, crimes that deserve punishment.

The book of Hebrews probably offers the best explanation for the various sacrifices offered on behalf of man. In the Old Testament animal sacrifices were offered. These sacrifices were offered on a regular basis. However, Hebrews 10:4 states "it is not possible that the blood of bulls and goats could take away sins." So what was the purpose of these sacrifices if they could not take away sins? Those sacrifices acted "as a reminder of sins" (Hebrews 10:3). You may have noted that when some people owe you money they often need to be reminded about it. The animal sacrifices kept before the people the fact that they had failed to live as they should.

Now this whole idea might sound a bit cruel if all God was offering his people was a yearly reminder that they were missing the mark. But throughout the Old Testament God was also sending prophets with the message that One was coming who would provide a way of forgiveness—someone who would be able to satisfy the demands of justice, as well as God's desire to forgive. That coming One was known by the Jews as the Messiah, the Hebrew equivalent of the Greek word *Christ*.

Of Jesus' sacrifice we are told "Christ was offered once to bear the sins of many" (Hebrews 9:28). Here we notice the purpose of the sacrifice of Jesus and how it differed from the previous animal sacrifices. When Jesus died it was to "bear the sins of many." In other words, he stood in our place. He took our punishment and satisfied the penalty for the crimes of the human race.

One of the best explanations of Jesus' bearing our sins was given by the famous British author Charles Dickens in *A Tale of Two Cities*. Set during the French Revolution, the book tells a story of the Tribunal sentencing Charles Darnay to death at the guillotine. But the lawyer Sydney Carton, who had for many years secretly loved Darnay's wife, Lucie, enters the prison and changes places with Darnay that Lucie might be spared the grief of losing her husband. Sydney Carton bore the punishment intended for another at the guillotine and uttered those famous words, "It is a far, far better thing that I do, than I have ever done."

This example loosely represents, as I believe Dickens intended, what Jesus did for us. He took our punishment, satisfying the guilty verdict our crimes had received.

What was wrong with the sacrifices of bulls and goats? Quite simply put, they could not take our place. If one person took the life of another person no one would think justice had been done if they executed the murderer's goat. From the biblical perspective an animal is not equal to a person. That is why the law God gave to Noah said, "Whoever sheds man's blood, by man his blood shall be shed."

Jesus was the only one qualified to take our place. Since all other people are themselves guilty of sin, it would not satisfy justice for one person to bear the punishment of another if, in fact, both were deserving of punishment anyway. But of Jesus the Bible says he was "in all points tempted as we are, yet without sin" (Hebrews 4:15). Jesus was qualified to bear our punishment because he was the only truly innocent human. This is why his sacrifice was offered only once. So just as Sydney Carton took the place of Charles Darnay out of his love for Lucie, so God allowed his only Son to take our place because of his love for us.

If I have failed to clarify these matters, let me know specifically what puzzles you.

Your friend,
Gene

SOUNDINGS

1. Why did God send the people a yearly reminder of their sinfulness?

2. Why was only Jesus able to bear the sins of the world?

3. How does the sacrifice of Jesus relate to salvation by grace?

WHAT DOES IT MEAN TO BE SAVED?

Chartings

Sin's Consequence

Spiritual Death

Rescued

Forgiven

July 10

Dear Lisa,

I hope you had an enjoyable 4th of July holiday.

As a teenager I heard a lot of religious people talking about being saved. I must confess that I was puzzled by what that meant. I later learned to think of being saved as being rescued. If someone falls out of a boat, for instance, and is saved from drowning, we know he was rescued. So when the Bible says we are saved by Jesus, it simply means Jesus rescued us.

When someone speaks of another being rescued, we usually ask, "Rescued from what?" What would have been the consequence had they not been rescued? In the case of falling out of a boat, one was saved from death by drowning.

Jesus saves or rescues people from the consequences of sin, often called *death* in the Bible. However, the death spoken of as resulting from sin is not merely a physical death; rather, it is a spiritual death. It is the destruction of one's relationship with God. And if one does not have a friendly relationship with God, he is not invited to live with God in eternity. So Jesus saves us from being eternally separated from God.

Being saved is another way of stating the idea of forgiveness. When one is forgiven for his sins, he has received salvation.

I realize this explanation is brief, but I hope you find it helpful.

Your friend,
Gene

SOUNDINGS

1. How does viewing salvation as being rescued lead to a better understanding of salvation?

2. When someone is rescued, he receives what he was about to lose. What do we receive when we are saved from sin?

3. What role do those who are rescued normally have in that rescue? How does that relate to our salvation from sin?

HELL AND A LOVING GOD

Chartings

- **Hell is Unpopular**
- **What Is Fair?**
- **Personal Bias**
- **God's Love**

August 1

Dear Lisa,

I understand that many women have false alarms and believe they have gone into labor, only to learn it was all a mistake. I sympathize with your embarrassment, but I suspect a dry run to the hospital is preferable to the possibility of giving birth in the back seat of your car.

The subject you have raised regarding the consequences of sin is one that has sent many Bible scholars to flight. When I wrote to you about the consequences of sin and eternal separation from God, I was not trying to gloss over the subject of hell. As I stated, my reply was brief; there was not time to address everything about life after death.

The Bible does talk about hell. Jesus spoke of it with greater frequency than any of his disciples did. He described it as a very unpleasant place. In a graphic description Jesus said one would rather lose his hand, foot, or eye than to be whole and eternally lost (Mark 9:42–48).

I have noted among people professing Christianity a tendency to reject the biblical teachings about hell. I recently read a survey taken among students at a church affiliated university in which over 90% of the respondents said they believed in heaven, but fewer than 50% said they believed in hell.

Your letter seemed to be asking me if there was not some way I could make what the Bible teaches about hell a bit more palatable than the traditional idea of eternal torment. I must tell you frankly that I cannot. I am aware that many are now claiming that when the Bible speaks of hell it is referring to a state of non-existence or annihilation, rather than a place of conscious, eternal punishment. This view basically teaches that the punishment of hell is being excluded from the reward of heaven. Such an idea does make the doctrine seem more tolerable. Such a view, however, does not do justice to the biblical evidence.

Lisa, there is no Bible doctrine I shrink from more than that of hell. If there were one Bible doctrine within my power to change, I suppose that would be the one. What the word of God says about hell is abhorrent. It is an abominable place; and it is God's wish that we find it so.

I am fully aware that the idea of there being a hell is a barrier to the belief of some seekers. But as I wrote to you early on in our correspondence, you deserve an honest answer and I do believe Jesus taught there is a place called hell. Theories that assert hell is a state where one ceases to exist seem very contrived in view of the clarity with which the Bible addresses the subject.

Most people who are offended by the concept of hell believe it is an idea unworthy of a Being who is claimed to be both loving and just. A loving God, I am told, would not concoct such a place. And it is deemed too harsh a punishment for sin, therefore some consider hell a concept beneath God.

When the philosophical dust has settled and all opinions have been offered, if one is going to claim the Bible is a revelation of the mind of God, then one must accept what it teaches and relinquish all personal bias on the matter.

I do admit, though, that even when a person determines to accept a biblical position that runs counter to his personal philosophy, he still must reconcile the two if he is going to find peace of mind.

Is hell an unfair or an unjust punishment for sin? Humans are not qualified to answer that question apart from revelation. We must remember that when human beings proclaim hell unfair because it is "cruel and unusual punishment," they are themselves sinners. Such a judgment is hardly unbiased. It is similar to allowing the convicted criminal to determine the punishment for his own crimes. It seems to me that a Being who stands outside the universe—capable of seeing the whole picture—himself without sin, is in a better position to know what is fair.

As for the objection that a loving God would not create a place like hell, I can't help but wonder how anyone is able to know what a loving God would do. If a person were claiming to know what a loving human being would do, I would say he has a good chance of being qualified to offer an opinion. But how could any of us know what a loving God would or would not do unless we ourselves are a loving God, or a loving God told us what he would do? I believe the Bible records the mind of a loving God telling us what he will do.

Since God sacrificed his only Son for us, how we can doubt his love?

I know the time of your delivery is drawing near, and I hope all continues to go well.

Your friend,
Gene

SOUNDINGS

1. Why do so many people believe in heaven but don't believe in hell even though the Bible speaks of both? (Matthew 10:28; 25:31–46; Mark 9:42–48).

2. When some deny the existence of hell because "it is something a loving God would never do," have they made a biblical argument? (cf. Revelation 21).

3. How could a human being know what a loving God would or would not do?

WHAT DOES IT MEAN TO BE BORN AGAIN?

Chartings

- "Born-Again Christian"?
- Old Man, New Man
- Water and Spirit
- New Creation

August 8

Dear Lisa,

Am I a born-again Christian? To answer bluntly: Yes, I have been born again. But I think I have some explaining to do.

From time to time I hear people place Christians in different categories, one of those categories being "born-again Christians." From the secular perspective, born-again Christians are the troublemakers—extremists. Born-again Christians are often spoken of in distinction to just plain old Christians, who are often considered to be more moderate in their views.

Frankly, I have never cared for the phrase "born-again Christian." I don't mind being spoken of as one who is born again, and I don't object to being called a Christian. I readily and without apology accept both descriptions. But I consider the phrase "born-again Christian" a useless redundancy. It is like saying someone is a female woman. All women are females and all Christians, according to the Bible, are born again.

The phrase "born again" goes back to a conversation Jesus had with a Jewish religious leader named Nicodemas, recorded in the third chapter of John. In the conversation Jesus tells Nicodemas that one must be born again in order to be a part of God's kingdom (John 3:3). He further explains that one is "born of water and the Spirit" (John 3:5), meaning they have been baptized and thus received the Holy Spirit.

The term "born again" has been given a kind of mystical quality by many, but it is really a very illustrative way of describing the idea that when one becomes a Christian he undergoes a change of life—becomes a new person. He gets a fresh start—becomes as a newborn baby.

"Born again" is only one of several Bible phrases describing a new state. In the book of 2 Corinthians the same idea is termed being a "new creation" (5:17). The book of Romans teaches that upon being baptized, Christians are to "walk in newness of life" (6:3–4). In the book of Ephesians another equivalent idea is that when one becomes a Christian he is to put off his former conduct, the "old man," and put on "the new man." The "new man" refers to conducting oneself as a follower of Jesus.

The instructions to put off and put on show that the change of life symbolized by terms like "born again" is not some mysterious instantaneous make over from above, but a daily effort on the part of the Christian to overcome life's temptations and behave in a godly manner.

You once asked me what Christians mean when they talk about being saved. Being saved, like being born again, is one of the many descriptions the Bible uses to illustrate various aspects of what it means to be a Christian.

I'm not sure who began using the terminology "born-again Christian," but I am sure the Christian community has not been served well by its use. From a biblical perspective, every Christian has been born again.

Your friend,
Gene

SOUNDINGS

1. Discuss the various ways you have heard the phrase "born again" used in conversation.

2. What picture does the phrase "born-again Christian" bring to the minds of people in the world?

3. Discuss the conversation between Nicodemus and Jesus. What did Nicodemus think Jesus meant by the phrase "born again"?

WHY CHRISTIANS ASSEMBLE

Chartings

- What Is Deserved
- Fellowship
- Duty
- Chore vs. Delight
- Praising God

August 15

Dear Lisa,

It was great to see you and your mom at church Sunday. You seem surprised that I am not shocked that you continue to attend our worship assemblies. Actually, I expect it. You and I have been corresponding for quite some time. While it is true I often speak with people whose interest in religion is a mere passing curiosity, few people could continue a dialogue for this long without genuine concern.

Why do Christians assemble? That is a good question, and there are many answers. Some Christians assemble because they have no choice. Perhaps Mom or Dad makes them go to church. I am sure there are some people at assemblies who would rather be somewhere else.

Some people assemble because it is a long-established habit. Some merely go through the motions of worship without much thought as to what they are doing or why they are doing it.

Based on your comment about some of the songs we sing, it is clear you were paying close attention. Yes, you are correct in noting that much of our assembly centers on praising God. However, it would be a mistake to assume that the whole thing makes God seem egotistical. From the Christian perspective it is simply giving God what he deserves.

Several months ago my wife and I attended a party at your house. You were very gracious and showed us around. You made it a point to mention some of the work Blaine had done. You showed us a piece of furniture he had made, and several other items that displayed his craftsmanship. Why did you spend all of that time praising your husband? Is it because he is egotistical and he demands you praise him regularly? Honestly, that thought never entered my mind. I assumed all of the praise was because you love him and are proud of him, and his skills deserve such praise. In fact, you seemed to derive much pleasure from praising him.

When an individual comes to know God, that person feels toward God very much like you feel toward your husband. For him, praising God is not a chore but a source of delight. He praises God to others for the same reason we "ooh" and "ah" over a beautiful sunset or magnificent waterfall. Praise is the natural reaction in such a situation. Silence would seem out of place. Christians believe they are merely offering God what he deserves when they praise him (Psalm 29:2; 96:8).

When parents expect obedience from their children, does that make the parents egomaniacs? Of course not. Children ought to obey their parents because good parents deserve to be obeyed. We worship God because it is his due. God is worthy of worship.

One of the great things about worship is that it not only involves discharging a duty toward a deserving God, but it provides a benefit for the worshipers. A second purpose of our assembly is to encourage and strengthen each other. In the book of Hebrews, Christian assemblies are said to be a time when we "consider one another in order to stir up love and good works" (10:24–25). Doing the right thing is not always easy. All of us are tempted to follow the path of least resistance. The assembly is a place where we draw courage and strength from one another to be the kind of people God wants us to be.

The word the Bible often uses to describe Christians' supporting one another is fellowship. Fellowship is the result of Christians' seeing one another as members of a big family. Jesus described his followers as a family. In fact, he said his spiritual family was even more important than his physical relatives (Matthew 12:46–50). It is this family concept that causes Christians to refer to one another as brother or sister. And just as you are now supporting your mother during her time of need, so Christians, being a family, support one another. A church assembly can be viewed as a big family gathering. Christians assemble to praise the Patriarch of the family and to encourage one another.

I hope I see you next Sunday.

Your friend,
Gene

SOUNDINGS

1. Why do you assemble for worship?

2. Do you think Christians today assemble more often or less often than first-century Christians? (Acts 2:40–47).

3. Do you have family feelings about others in the church? Explain your answer.

INFANT BAPTISM

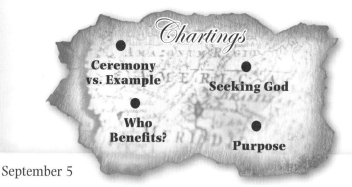

Chartings

Ceremony
vs. Example

Seeking God

Who
Benefits?

Purpose

September 5

Dear Lisa,

Congratulations! October 1 will be a very special day for you and Blaine from this day forward.

Sandra is beautiful. I am always amazed by the hands of babies—so tiny and delicate. I know you were concerned because she was a few weeks early, but it doesn't seem to have created any complications.

Thank you for inviting me to visit while you were in the hospital. Your mom surely did enjoy holding the baby.

I must admit I was rather surprised at your inquires about christening Sandra. I have witnessed a few of these ceremonies and they can be beautiful and quite moving. However, I hope you will understand when I tell you that we do not perform such ceremonies for the simple reason that we have no record of infants being baptized in the New Testament. Baptism was reserved for penitent believers (Mark 16:16; Acts 2:36–38). We would, however, be delighted to have special prayer for her.

Still, I was quite excited when you asked about a christening for Sandra. It probably sounds strange to you that I would be happy you desire to perform a religious rite not practiced by the fellowship to which I belong, but to me it signals your movement toward God.

Lisa, I'm not sure of your motive for wanting to christen the baby. If you are wanting to do it for Sandra's benefit, then you need to ask yourself how Sandra will benefit from the ceremony. Most groups that practice infant baptism view it as something done for the parent's benefit. If your desire is to provide her with a foundation upon which she can build her own relationship with God, then I think you know an infant ceremony will not accomplish that goal.

Children do not learn to value something simply because of a ceremony performed in their infancy. They learn to value things that are an integral part of the daily family life. They learn to honor things their parents honor. Moses commanded the Israelites to teach their children the commands of God. "You shall teach them diligently to your children, and shall talk to them when you sit in your house, when you walk by the way, when you lie down, and when you rise up" (Deuteronomy 6:7). Frankly, I think the most beneficial thing you can do to help Sandra is something you are already working at, and that is to establish your own connection with God. If your little girl grows up seeing her parents' daily actions being influenced by their belief in God, then there is a much better chance she also will seek God.

Christening ceremonies have a certain sentimental beauty, but teaching Sandra about God is something you and Blaine must work at as long as she is in your house.

Congratulations on the birth of your baby!

Your friend,
Gene

SOUNDINGS

1. How could being baptized as an infant give one a desire to have a closer relationship with God?

2. Have you ever attended a christening ceremony? What took place? What was said?

3. Study what the Bible teaches about baptism. Can an infant do all of the things required of baptized people? (Mark 16:16; Acts 2:38).

Questions about Salvation

Religious Division

Chartings

- Church of Choice?
- Jesus' Prayer
- Bible Pattern
- Confusion

September 22

Dear Lisa,

I was elated to see your whole family at church Sunday. I hope all of the people making a fuss over the baby didn't make you too nervous.

I believe you are right about your mom appearing rather feeble, but she is still strong in spirit and her face was full of joy as she sat with you, Blaine, and Sandra at church Sunday.

I am glad you are feeling more at ease with the idea of God and organized religion. I also sympathize with your puzzlement over the great number of churches. It really is a confusing situation.

God never intended that believers be divided into many different churches. The fragmentation you see is purely the work of the human race.

Jesus prayed that all who believe in him "may be one" (John 17:21). I was impressed with your observation that divisions among believers have turned many against Christianity; Jesus himself said the same thing. He prayed that all of his followers "may be one . . . that the world may believe that You [the Father] sent me." Unity among believers promotes belief. Clearly then, division promotes unbelief.

As to what can be done about all of the divisions, if I had the answer to that one I would indeed be a wise man. It seems to me, however, the greatest problem is that the various churches have become comfortable with division. More than comfortable, a divided Christendom has actually become virtuous with slogans such as "Attend the church of your choice."

I understand religious division when one church thinks the other is guilty of beliefs or actions that destroy fellowship with God. Such divisions are even sanctioned in Scripture (2 John 9–11). What I do not understand are divisions that leave the impression that their differences are not really that big a deal, so just "attend the church of your choice" because "one is as good as another." Churches that really believe one is good as another ought to close their doors and join up with one another.

If all of the various churches really are just one big happy family, then the least we should do is meet together for worship. A family that can't stay in the same room for a couple of hours a week is in a pretty sad condition. My point is, though many are fond of saying things like, "Attend the church of your choice," I don't believe they are really as broad-minded as they wish to appear.

But since religious organizations do not seem all that interested in ending the divisions, the believer is left with the enormous task of looking for a church he believes teaches and behaves as the Bible says the church should. The only thing I know to tell you is to read your Bible and look for a church that follows what it teaches. Be especially mindful of things that appear unique to a religious body. Few people like to be looked upon as different or strange. Therefore, when a religious body is willing to risk being viewed as rather quirky, the prudent thing to do is to ask why the difference exists. How shocking it might be to learn that those with the unusual habit are, in fact, the ones following the Bible, while the others have been diverted into following human tradition. We can ill afford to lightly write off as a flake everyone who is different.

I'm sorry we religious people have made your search so difficult.

Your friend,
Gene

SOUNDINGS

1. List some practices of the church you attend that might seem unusual, especially to visitors.

2. Have you ever been asked to defend a certain practice that is different from most churches? How did you respond?

3. Discuss other unusual practices of the church where you attend. How would you explain them to others?

COMING TO BELIEF

Chartings

Sustaining Relationship

Teaching in Death

Comfort in Suffering

A Better Place

September 30

Dear Lisa,

Even when death is expected, we are never prepared when it comes. Your mother was a very special lady. There was something about being in her presence that made everyone around her want to be a better person. Though her achievements were many, she was most proud of being a godly wife and mother. It is difficult to imagine an assembly of the church without her. I am sure her absence will bring to mind the way Jonathan felt when he said of his dear friend David: "Tomorrow is the New Moon; and you will be missed, because your seat will be empty" (1 Samuel 20:18). Her death is a big loss for everyone who knew her, and especially for you and your family. However, she left this world having lived to hold her granddaughter—and name sake. She also saw you starting down the path that will hopefully, one day, lead to faith.

Of course, as a Christian her life has just begun in a place where the Bible teaches there are no more tears, nor is there any pain (Revelation 21:4). Pain is something she had more of than her share during the past few months. No wonder we call heaven a "better place." When our suffering is the greatest, Christians find some measure of comfort in the words of Paul: "For I consider that the sufferings of this present time are not worthy to be compared with the glory which shall be revealed in us" (Romans 8:18).

You believe it was your mother's relationship with God that sustained her during her waning days, and now you find yourself craving that same kind of relationship. How touching. Even in death your mother is teaching important lessons about faith.

Of course, I would be honored to speak at your mother's funeral. It will be difficult to find words that will do justice to her life. She lived and died a lady of faith.

Your friend,
Gene

SOUNDINGS

1. When Christians die they go to be with God. Does this mean it is wrong to cry at the funeral of a Christian? (John 11:35).

2. Read 1 Thessalonians 4:13–18. How is death different for Christians?

3. How is the death of a Christian different for the loved ones left behind?

DRAWING CLOSER TO GOD

Chartings

- Reason vs. Emotion
- Spiritual Warfare
- Faith Is the Winner
- Declare Unbelief

October 6

Dear Lisa,

When we spoke on the phone the other day, I couldn't help but notice that what began in your mind as a brief skirmish between faith in God and unbelief has escalated into a gigantic war. I know old ways of thinking are difficult to dislodge, but I cannot help but think that God has won this battle. You are living what Paul spoke of when he wrote: "For though we walk in the flesh, we do not war according to the flesh. For the weapons of our warfare are not carnal but mighty in God for pulling down strongholds, casting down arguments and every high thing that exalts itself against the knowledge of God, bringing every thought into captivity to the obedience of Christ" (2 Corinthians 10:3–5).

All the arguments have been answered; the only thing needed is for you to finally declare him the victor in your heart. Then, I believe, you can move forward with your spiritual life. When I say it is time for you to declare a victor, I understand the immediate reaction is to say such sounds too artificial. We tend to believe that in order for a victory between competing ideas to be legitimate and decisive it should take place of its own accord. We believe it ought to be like falling in love, it just happens. However, it seems to me that the battle you are now fighting is not one of reason. You have set forth your reasons for not believing, and you have admitted that those reasons have been answered. Reason is now on the side of faith. It is not reason that faith is now battling within you, but emotion. And I believe it is possible that your current confusion is the natural condition of all who allow emotions to drive their lives. There comes a time when we must tell both imagination and emotion to let go of the wheel.

Both the Bible and reason support the idea that there is a moment in time when victory should be declared. In the Bible we often read of people who came out of unbelief with a dramatic declaration. You remind me of the man who brought his sick son to Jesus to be healed. Jesus told the father, "If you can believe, all things are possible to him who believes." The man cried out, "Lord I believe; help my unbelief" (Mark 9:23–24). It is natural that unbelief should continue to storm the walls faith has been building in your mind. May I suggest that you declare your belief and ask God to help you with your unbelief?

Lisa, I have been a Christian for some 20 years. To this day I continue to have that odd thought, "What if all of this is not true? What if there is no God and this life is all there is?" But I tell you frankly that such ideas do not enter my mind when I am thinking in a calm rational manner about the Bible and Christianity. Those thoughts are the product of a moment of turmoil. Those thoughts invade my fortress of faith when it seems like things around me are falling apart. During those moments I must ask myself, "Have you come to possess some new piece of information that convinces you Jesus is not the Son of God?" The answer, of course, is no. So I declare faith the winner. Or, as John put it, "And this is the victory that has overcome the world—our faith" (1 John 5:4).

Please do not misunderstand me. I am not trying to get you to declare something you do not believe. I am not asking you to be phony. I am simply saying that perhaps you need to try telling emotion and unbelief where to get off.

Your friend,
Gene

SOUNDINGS

1. Read the following passages and ask yourself if the idea of finally ending the debate by declaring one's faith seems false or phony (Acts 2:37; 9:6; 8:36; John 9:38; 20:28).

2. Have you had moments of doubt about God? What did you do?

3. Are moments of doubt unusual among Christians? Why or why not?

BECOMING A CHRISTIAN

Chartings

Acceptance or Rejection

Jesus Is Son of God

Examples in Acts

Saved upon Confession?

Repentance, Baptism

October 11

Dear Lisa,

You cannot imagine how excited I was when I read your letter. A good deal of mail had accumulated while I was away, but I opened your letter first because you seem to be growing more and more comfortable with faith in Jesus as the Son of God. To learn that you have come to believe is just the information I had hoped the letter would contain.

The encounter you had with an associate at work is interesting. Having known you for some time, I am sure she was a bit surprised when you shared with her your recently-arrived-at conviction that Jesus is the Son of God. It is wonderful that you were willing to publicly profess that belief. Jesus said those who deny him before others would themselves be denied by him before the Father (Matthew 10:32–33).

It is what happened next that leaves me rather puzzled. At the instigation of your friend you bowed your head and confessed to God that you were a sinner badly in need of forgiveness, and that you were giving your life to him. That is a touching sentiment, and there is much good in the willingness to admit needing God's forgiveness. Humility is important when approaching God. "God resists the proud, but gives grace to the humble" (James 4:6).

Where I get lost is when your colleague told you that you were a Christian as a result of that prayer. The reason I am puzzled is because if you in fact were saved at that very moment, then it is unlike anything I have ever read in the Bible. I hope you will take the time to read the book of Acts in your New Testament. That book contains several examples of people who were told what God expected them to do to be saved. Interestingly enough, the accounts are all virtually the same insofar as what the individuals did in order to receive forgiveness. I conclude from this that there is a specific procedure set forth by God that all follow in order to receive forgiveness of sins. I do not recall any example in which a person, having come to belief, was told to pray to God in order to be a Christian. I would feel very uncomfortable if what I did in order to be saved was different from these examples.

I know you have a tendency to want to figure these things out for yourself rather than have the information handed to you. I even understand why you feel that way, for most people have greater confidence in a conviction if they feel they reached it on their own. When we receive a lot of guidance, we sometimes wonder if the conviction is ours or that of our guide. Please forgive me if I seem a bit too helpful in this matter, but your soul is at stake and I am afraid I cannot be nonchalant about something this important.

As you know, Jesus spent about three years with his disciples, teaching them the things they needed to know to spread the knowledge of salvation to the world. After his resurrection the Bible records many of the Lord's appearances to his followers. During the final appearance, after which he ascended back to heaven, he gave his followers a mission. This event is recorded in Matthew, Mark, and Luke, and it is often called the Great Commission.

As is often the case, each account provides a little information not given in the others, so it is necessary to put them all together to learn the entirety of their mission. Here are the passages in question.

Matthew records: "All authority has been given to Me in heaven and on earth. Go therefore and make disciples of all the nations, baptizing them in the name of the Father and of the Son and of the Holy Spirit, teaching them to observe all things that I have commanded you; and lo, I am with you always, even to the end of the age" (Matthew 28:18–20).

Mark's record is "Go into all the world and preach the gospel to every creature. He who believes and is baptized will be saved; but he who does not believe will be condemned" (Mark 16:15–16).

Luke says: "Thus it is written, and thus it was necessary for the Christ to suffer and to rise from the dead the third day, and that repentance and remission of sins should be preached in His name to all nations, beginning at Jerusalem. And you are witnesses of these things" (Luke 24:46–48).

Lisa, when we put all of these accounts together we note that the disciples' mission was to preach the good news concerning the death and resurrection of Jesus. Those people who believed the message preached by the disciples were urged to turn away from sin and be baptized, resulting in their being saved, or receiving remission of sins. To put a fine point on it, in order to be saved, a believer must turn from sin and be baptized.

Though I believe I have correctly correlated this information, I realize that some might wonder if I have made a mistake in the way I have pieced things together. Fortunately there is a way to test my handling of this material. You may remember that in algebra, after solving for X, you had to plug your answer into the equation to see if the solution was correct. We have a similar situation in the Bible. The accounts we have just examined in Matthew, Mark, and Luke are Jesus telling the disciples what they are to do after he is gone. But in the book of Acts we have recorded what the disciples actually did. One looks forward while the other looks backward. One is future tense and the other is past tense. If I have correctly understood what Jesus told his disciples to do in Matthew, Mark, and Luke, then it ought to be reflected in the book of Acts.

In Acts 2 as the apostles are gathered in Jerusalem they receive the Holy Spirit. The result is that Peter preaches to the crowd present in Jerusalem for the Pentecost feast. Peter gives a concluding summary of his message in Acts 2:36: "Therefore let all the house of Israel know assuredly that God has made this Jesus, whom you crucified, both Lord and Christ." Clearly, Peter has preached the gospel as Jesus had commanded. In verse 37 we learn that many in his audience believe what he taught about Jesus, for they cry out, "Men and brethren, what shall we do?" Peter tells them to "repent, and let every one of you be baptized in the name of Jesus Christ for the remission of sins; and you shall receive the gift of the Holy Spirit."

Peter's answer corresponds precisely with what Jesus said they should do. He didn't tell them to pray for forgiveness; rather, he told them to turn away from sin [repent] and be baptized in order to receive remission of sins [be saved].

Lisa, if you follow the pattern set forth in the Bible you will get the result God promised—salvation, forgiveness of sins. The Bible teaches that Christians ought to pray, but nowhere does it teach that one ought to pray in order to become a Christian.

I know what I have written has filled you with questions. I can even anticipate some of your questions. But when all of the questions have been asked and discussed, it all comes down to one simple matter: What does the Bible teach? If the Bible teaches salvation is the result of a penitent believer's being baptized, then what is there left to discuss? Furthermore, if this is what the Bible teaches, why would anyone reject it?

I hope to hear from you soon.

Your friend,
Gene

SOUNDINGS

1. What are some of the most common questions people have after learning that the Bible does not teach one to pray for forgiveness, but instead to repent and be baptized?

2. Does the Bible seem unclear about repentance and baptism coming before salvation? Try to find a passage where salvation comes before baptism.

3. Do the things we have noted about salvation in the Bible agree with what you did to be saved?

GRACE AND FAITH

October 17

Dear Lisa,

Your recent letter reminded me how far we have come in our discussions. In the beginning your letters were from a skeptic's perspective. Now we are investigating theological issues regarding the salvation of the soul. It is simply amazing.

Your aunt expressed a view that is quite common among those who believe in Jesus. It is obvious that believers are divided into many religious bodies, each of them representing some teaching peculiar to themselves. But it is indeed unfortunate that one of the areas of disagreement regards what one must do to receive salvation. It is one of the most fundamental matters of Christianity. Jesus himself said he came to "seek and save that which was lost" (Luke 19:10). You would think this is one of the areas we ought to be able to get right.

I agree with your aunt when she states: "Salvation is by grace, not by works. You can't earn salvation." From the description of your conversation, I suspect where we differ is in the matter of what constitutes work? In examining this question it is of the utmost importance that we define our terms correctly, otherwise we find ourselves facing biblical data that appears conflicting. Let me show you what I mean.

You and I have already discussed the biblical idea of grace. The blessings we receive from God are by grace, which simply means we do not deserve the blessings. Blessings from God are unearned gifts. Though this idea is taught in many places in both the Old and New Testaments, it is most clearly set forth in Ephesians 2:8–9: "For by grace you have been saved through faith, and that not of yourselves; it is the gift of God, not of works, lest anyone should boast." The teaching here is quite plain: no one is saved because human efforts have placed God in his debt. In fact, not only have we not earned salvation, but other places in the Bible indicate that God made the way of salvation possible even while we lived in overt rebellion against him. "But God demonstrates His own love toward us, in that while we were still sinners, Christ died for us" (Romans 5:8). Clearly God owes us nothing. Since all blessings from God are given by grace, it is not surprising to find statements rejecting the possibility of receiving salvation due to personal merit.

Strangely enough, however, there are a number of biblical statements indicating that our actions do have something to do with whether or not we are in a right relationship with God. Jesus said, "Not everyone who says to Me, 'Lord, Lord,' shall enter the kingdom of heaven, but he who does the will of My Father in heaven" (Matthew 7:21). Even the writings of Paul, which many believe contain the clearest defense of salvation by faith, indicate the necessity of works. To the Philippians he wrote: "Work out your own salvation with fear and trembling" (Philippians 2:12). To the Corinthians he wrote, "For we must all appear before the judgment seat of Christ, that each one may receive the things done in the body, according to what he has done, whether good or bad" (2 Corinthians 5:10; cf Romans 2:16).

The reconciliation to these apparent contradictions is simple: obedience to God is not considered a work of merit. Obedience is necessary if one is to be pleasing to God.

Works of merit and works of obedience are very different. An excellent example of this is in how the New Testament writers refer to Abraham. In Romans 4:2–4 Paul writes that salvation is by faith and not by works of merit. "For if Abraham was justified by works, he has something to boast about, but not before God. For what does the Scripture say? Abraham believed God, and it was accounted to him for righteousness. Now to him who works, the wages are not counted as grace but as debt." Yet, James writes this about Abraham: "Was not Abraham our father justified by works when he offered Isaac his son on the altar? Do you see that faith was working together with his works, and by works faith was made perfect? And the Scripture was fulfilled which says, 'Abraham believed God, and it was accounted to him for righteousness.' And he was called the friend of God. You see then that a man is justified by works, and not by faith only" (James 2:21–24). One writer says God blessed Abraham because of his faith and not because he deserved to be blessed. Another writer says Abraham was "justified by works, and not by faith only." Both writers even quote the same Old Testament passage to prove their case. Apparently obeying God does not qualify as a meritorious work.

Lisa, there is no contradiction in these accounts; the writers are referring to different kinds of works. Romans teaches the impossibility of being saved by one's personal goodness apart from the sacrifice of Jesus. James teaches that a saving faith is faith that obeys God. God does not owe salvation to anyone. An obedient person is simply fulfilling the natural result of his faith. Jesus said it clearly: "So likewise you, when you have done all those things which you are commanded, say, 'We are unprofitable servants. We have done what was our duty to do'" (Luke 17:10).

When Ephesians 2:8 states "for by grace have you been saved through faith," it is teaching that our salvation involves two individuals, each with a different role. God offers salvation by grace (unmerited favor). The saved receive that salvation by means of faith in God, a trust which includes obedience.

Your aunt objected to the idea that baptism is essential to salvation, believing it to be a work of merit. However, since the Bible clearly teaches baptism is necessary for salvation (Mark 16:15–16; Acts 2:38; 22:16; Romans 6:3–4; 1 Peter 3:21), one must conclude that baptism is not a meritorious action; rather, it is an act of faith obeying God.

I hope this explanation helps you in your deliberations.

Your friend,
Gene

P.S. I would be more than happy to discuss this with your aunt if she would like.

SOUNDINGS

1. Compare Joshua 6:2 and Hebrews 11:30. Was Jericho a gift from God? Is it possible for God to give a gift conditionally? Does a gift cease to be a gift if one must meet conditions to receive it?

2. Explain the difference between the works Paul wrote about in Ephesians 2:8–9 and those referred to by James in James 2.

3. What does Luke 17:10 say about our obedience to God and meriting salvation?

GOD: THE FATHER OR A 500-POUND GORILLA?

Chartings

Limitations of Fear

Beyond Commandments

Provider

Intimidation Factor

Father and Child

October 21

Dear Lisa,

Praise God! Since I have come to know you I have seen you grow ever closer to God. In the past year you have suffered through times of great sorrow and experienced joy beyond measure, but through it all you have grown nearer to God. Thank you for letting me have a part in your journey to salvation.

Cindy and I have been praying for this moment for such a long time. It was so sweet to hear you say those words: "I believe Jesus Christ is the Son of God." Baptism is always an emotional moment, but I cannot recall seeing tears flow quite as freely as they did at your immersion. At least none of us had to feel self-conscious about our tears. The way Blaine was crying, I half expected him to ask to be baptized. It will be my prayer that your baptism will be only the first in your family, with Blaine and Sandra one day following. I guess the only one who wasn't weeping was Sandra.

Please know this: your journey has only begun. You now have the rest of your life to build and nurture your bond with him.

You have turned the tables on me by asking about my relationship with God. I am accustomed to being the one who asks the questions. This letter will be rather lengthy, but it is the best I could do at putting to paper my thoughts about my relationship with God.

Consider this very strange question: What does a 500-pound Gorilla do? Answer: Anything he wishes.

I am not going to presume to speak for others, but I must admit my attitude toward God has often been like one's attitude toward a 500-pound gorilla. You respect, fear, and obey a 500-pound gorilla because the alternative is an angry gorilla.

Now I know the Bible presents God as loving and merciful, wanting what is best for us; but I don't think you can or should totally escape the intimidation factor. Let me put it this way. Here you are holding a big bunch of bananas when along comes this 500-pound animal and his trainer. The trainer, who is very reassuring, says, "Oh, don't worry about him; he's perfectly harmless. Why I've never seen him hurt a fly"—as if the gorilla's attitude toward insects were a present concern. Despite the trainer's assurances, if the big gorilla extends his hand toward my bananas I'm handing them over—not because he is kind, but because he is a 500-pound gorilla.

The point is obvious: sometimes we obey God because we are afraid not to obey him. That is not the best reason for obeying him, but it is a reason. "The fear of the Lord is the beginning of knowledge" (Proverbs 1:7). The key word here is *beginning*. The strength of obedience out of fear is its immediate effect. Certainly, obedience out of love is superior in its motive (1 Corinthians 13:13), but love takes time to mature. In the beginning fear will do just fine. Who knows? Maybe if I had time to hang out with the 500-pound gorilla for a few days, I might come to share my bananas with him because I appreciate his warm and sensitive ways. But it doesn't take any time at all to grasp the fear angle. There is a lot to be said for immediate results.

But fear also has very definite limitations, which is why it is only the *beginning* of knowledge. For one thing, fear is temporary, and when fear is gone the obedience usually goes with it. But the temporary nature of fear is not its greatest limitation. Obedience gained *exclusively* through fear tends to produce resentment. If I surrender my bananas out of fear, I resent giving them up. Obeying God's commands purely out of fear makes the commands seem burdensome, which is exactly what the Bible says they are not (1 John 5:3). You see, the problem isn't with the commands; rather, the problem is one's attitude toward God. At least, this is how it was for me.

Lisa, your statement that it seemed difficult to conceive of God as more than a character described in the Bible, with no real substance, was one to which I could relate. It is quite possible to come away from the Bible seeing God as merely a maker of rules. It is possible to have religion without having a sense of relationship with God. Most Christians who are dominated by fear have religion without any sense of relationship. Unfortunately, for many years I was like that—a deeply religious person with no real sense of a relationship with God. I knew what the Bible taught about God, theologically speaking. I understood he was all-powerful and all-knowing, but none of those facts really provided a handle by which I could grasp God and say I knew him.

A key for me was finally figuring out there was something beyond the commandments—a family relationship. The Bible presents Christians as part of the family of God. When we are baptized we are added to God's family, the church. We become his children by adoption. That is why Christians often refer to one another as brother and sister. When I finally grasped the fatherhood concept of God, things really changed for me.

But for whatever reasons, it took me a while to catch on to the family concept. I had to come to know God as my Father rather than as a powerful and intimidating stranger. I can't explain why that took me so long. I knew the Scriptures called him Father. But one day it dawned on me as I was reading the Sermon on the Mount. In Matthew chapter 6 Jesus gives his followers an example of prayer. His example begins in verse 9 with these words: "Our Father in heaven." In teaching others about this prayer I had always been quick to point out that Jesus was teaching us to address God as our Father. I think it was that very wording that kept me from understanding the power of those simple words. To me this was teaching how we address God, but Jesus was talking about our relationship with God. You address a business letter; you talk to your Father. For many years I was saying, "Heavenly Father" as I began my prayers, but I was thinking, "Dear Sir." I was addressing a letter to a John Doe. I was putting in a requisition, placing an order, rather than asking my dad. I was praying to a stranger! I doubt I am the only one who has had this problem.

My relationship with God began to fall into place once I started to grasp this idea. Our dad is someone who gives orders. He's bigger than we are and he's stronger than we are, yet we manage to do his will without resentment. Because of the relationship we have with our dad we are able to take commands from him without feeling bitter. In the Bible God is presented as our Father. Why? Because he wants us to understand that the sense of relationship we have with our dads here on earth is the same feeling of affection God has toward his children. It is through that same parent-child relationship he wants us to come to think of him.

Not only is God spoken of as our Father—in the sense of being someone we can talk to—but he is also presented to us as a provider. In the context where we are told to "seek first the kingdom of God" (Matthew 6:33), our Father in heaven is being portrayed as our Provider. The idea of God as our Father-Provider is summarized in these words: "Therefore do not worry saying, 'What shall we eat?' or 'What shall we drink?' or 'What shall we wear?' For after all these things the Gentiles seek. For your heavenly Father knows that you need all these things" (Matthew 6:31–32).

I was blessed with a happy childhood. It never occurred to me to run away from home. Why run away from a place where all your needs are taken care of? And very high on a child's necessary list is food. My life was so carefree that I can remember only one time thinking how important it was to know there was always going to be supper, and that was when one of my best friends ran away from home.

I grew up in West Palm Beach, Florida, in a housing subdivision on the banks of the Palm Beach Canal, a huge canal that helped drain the Everglades into the ocean. Alligators and ducks were abundant in the canal's wildlife. One day I went to play with my friend Denny Johns. You can imagine my shock when Mr. Johns calmly said: "He's run away from home, so if you want to see him he's down on the canal bank around back."

I found Denny just in time because he was well on his way, having gone at least three houses down the canal. And I could tell he had thought the situation out because he had all of his provisions in a backpack. But even more important was the bag of marbles and the slingshot he held in his hands. I sat down beside my friend: "Denny what are you doing?" And he said, "I'm running away from home." He was visibly upset; his eyes were still red from his tears. I asked him why he was running away and the story tumbled out. He was tired of the way things were at home. He was tired of taking those commands. So there we both sat at the ripe old age of 11. Since I wasn't as upset as Denny was, it was clear I was going to have to be the practical one. The first thought that came to my mind was food. "What are you going to eat?" I asked calmly. Without a word he simply held up his bag of marbles and slingshot. I said, "What are you going to do with those?" He replied, "I'm going to shoot ducks and eat them." This plan, quite frankly, didn't sound too promising to me. As was usually the case, there was a duck swimming in the canal, so I challenged my friend. "Denny," I said, "shoot that duck." Denny confidently fitted a marble into his slingshot, pulled back on the elastic, took careful aim, and missed. He shot all around that duck but never hit it. Denny then did the only sensible thing one does in these situations—he picked up his marbles and went home.

I learned from Denny the importance of my parents as providers. That is what God is to us. He is our Father; he provides for us.

Another important idea that comes with knowing God as your Father is the confidence that whatever he asks of you is for your own good. Jesus put it this way, "Or what man is there among you who, if his son asks for bread, will give him a stone? Or if he asks for a fish, will he give him a serpent? If you then, being evil, know how to give good gifts to your children, how much more will your Father who is in heaven give good things to those who ask Him!" (Matthew 7:9–11).

Now, Lisa, here is the point. Didn't you have confidence that when your dad told you to do something, he told you to do it because he thought it was in your best interest? I didn't ask you if you thought he always knew what was best for you. We know every kid who reaches the age of 12 suddenly doubts his parents' knowledge of anything. But there was one thing most of us kids did believe. Even when we didn't think they *knew* what was best for us, we always believed our parents *thought* they were doing what was best for us. Children often do that which is asked of them, even when they have doubts, because a sincere, loving person asked them to do it. It's called trust. Another term the Bible uses for this trust is faith. When our conception of God is that of Father, we trust that what he asks of us is in our best interest, even if we don't understand how.

Along with the idea that I need to have a sense that God is my Father-Provider and that he knows how to give good gifts to his children, I must also have a sense of my own childishness. If God is my Father, then I am a child. When I was a small child my dad was God, as far as I was concerned. I do not say that blasphemously. That is the way God set it up—the way he intended it should be. If it could be known, my dad knew it. He could do anything and fix everything. And so when dad said to do something, how could I argue with him?

But then a major problem developed: I began to grow up. And you know what happens when you begin to grow up. When you think you are grown-up, you are suddenly convinced that Mom and Dad really don't know any more than you do. Suddenly you are not quite as willing to do what Dad says because you begin to see yourself as his equal; you're a grownup, too.

Regrettably, I have sometimes perceived my relationship with my Father in heaven this way. There are times when I don't see myself as a child, but as a grown-up. It's not that I think God's way isn't best, but I sometimes am convinced my way is all right, too. "Maybe my way isn't as good as God's," I tell myself, "but my way is good enough." That is grown-up thinking. However, Scripture says it is not in man to direct his own steps (Jeremiah 10:23; Proverbs 14:12)

In the Bible we are told God came to Solomon and said, "Ask! What shall I give you?" What an opportunity! God had given Solomon a blank check and told him to fill in the amount. Solomon chose wisdom, saying, "I am a little child; I do not know how to go out or come in" (1 Kings 3:5–7). Solomon recognized he was a child and God was an adult. I have an idea this is an example of what Jesus meant when he said, "Therefore whoever humbles himself as this little child is the greatest in the kingdom of heaven" (Matthew

18:4). Jesus was telling us we must have a sense of our own child-ishness. We must get back to looking up to God in awe as we used to look up to our dads. Our heavenly Father really does know every-thing and really can fix anything. Believing this, I must conclude that there is only one way to do things—his way. I cannot conclude that his way is best but my way is okay. Why should I think there is only one way to do things? Because God is my Father and I am a child, and I do not know how to go out and I do not know how to come in.

This, Lisa, is something beyond the commandments. When I get a sense of the fatherhood of God and of my own childishness, then I find myself doing the commandments because my Father feels the same affection for me that I feel for my own children—that you and Blaine feel for Sandra—and he gave the commandments. Because he is my Father I know he will not command me to do something that is not in my best interest anymore than I would knowingly tell my children to do something I thought would be destructive.

I have found that religion without relationship is simply a joy-less life of taking orders from someone that is bigger than me, and stronger than me, and can hurt me. Parents need to consider how they feel toward their own children and realize that God has simi-lar feelings toward his children. And the trust young children have in their parents is the same trust the parents should have in God. Knowing God as your Father, and not as a 500-pound gorilla, is something beyond the commandments.

Writing this letter has certainly been good for me. I hope you find it helpful as you continue on your Christian journey.

Your brother in Christ,
Gene